D1548892

Tracy, Brian.
Find your balance
point

MAR 0 5 2018

DISCARD

·

**FIND
YOUR
BALANCE
POINT**

·

ALSO BY CHRISTINA STEIN AND BRIAN TRACY

Kiss That Frog!

OTHER BOOKS BY BRIAN TRACY

Eat That Frog!

Maximum Achievement

Advanced Selling Strategies

The 100 Absolutely Unbreakable Laws of Business Success

21 Success Secrets of Self-Made Millionaires

Focal Point

Victory!

Create Your Own Future

Goals!

TurboStrategy

Be a Sales Superstar

Change Your Thinking, Change Your Life

Million Dollar Habits

Time Power

Getting Rich Your Own Way

TurboCoach

The Psychology of Selling

Something for Nothing

The Art of Closing the Sale

Crunch Point

The Way to Wealth

FIND YOUR BALANCE POINT

•

Brian Tracy
Christina Stein

Berrett–Koehler Publishers, Inc.
a BK Life book

Copyright © 2015 by Brian Tracy and Christina Stein.

All rights reserved. No part of this publication may be reproduced, distributed, or transmitted in any form or by any means, including photocopying, recording, or other electronic or mechanical methods, without the prior written permission of the publisher, except in the case of brief quotations embodied in critical reviews and certain other noncommercial uses permitted by copyright law. For permission requests, write to the publisher, addressed "Attention: Permissions Coordinator," at the address below.

Berrett-Koehler Publishers, Inc.
1333 Broadway, Suite 1000
Oakland, CA 94612-1921
Tel: (510) 817-2277   Fax: (510) 817-2278   www.bkconnection.com

Ordering Information

Quantity sales. Special discounts are available on quantity purchases by corporations, associations, and others. For details, contact the "Special Sales Department" at the Berrett-Koehler address above.

Individual sales. Berrett-Koehler publications are available through most bookstores. They can also be ordered directly from Berrett-Koehler: Tel: (800) 929-2929; Fax: (802) 864-7626; www.bkconnection.com.

Orders for college textbook/course adoption use. Please contact Berrett-Koehler: Tel: (800) 929-2929; Fax: (802) 864-7626.

Orders by U.S. trade bookstores and wholesalers. Please contact Ingram Publisher Services, Tel: (800) 509-4887; Fax: (800) 838-1149; E-mail: customer.service@ingram publisherservices.com; or visit www.ingrampublisherservices.com/Ordering for details about electronic ordering.

Berrett-Koehler and the BK logo are registered trademarks of Berrett-Koehler Publishers, Inc.

Printed in the United States of America

Berrett-Koehler books are printed on long-lasting acid-free paper. When it is available, we choose paper that has been manufactured by environmentally responsible processes. These may include using trees grown in sustainable forests, incorporating recycled paper, minimizing chlorine in bleaching, or recycling the energy produced at the paper mill.

Library of Congress Cataloging-in-Publication Data
Tracy, Brian.
  Find your balance point : how to clarify your priorities, simplify your
life, and achieve more / Brian Tracy and Christina Stein.—First edition.
    pages cm
  Includes bibliographical references and index.
  ISBN 978-1-62656-572-2 (hardcover : alk. paper)
  1. Goal (Psychology) 2. Time management. 3. Values. 4. Self-realization.
I. Stein, Christina Tracy. II. Title.
  BF505.G6T727 2015
  158.1—dc23   2015018825

FIRST EDITION
19 18 17 16 15   10 9 8 7 6 5 4 3 2 1

Copyediting & proofreading by PeopleSpeak
Book design & composition by Beverly Butterfield, Girl of the West Productions
Cover design by Ian Koviak, The Book Designers
Cover images by Shutterstock
Photo of Christina Stein by Louis Yansen
Indexing by Rachel Rice

This book is dedicated to my mother, Barbara, and to my two best friends, Mina Neuberg and Niki Rein. These three incredible women, who have shared my journey to achieve balance, loved and supported me along the way, and have taught me the blessing of true friendship.

CHRISTINA

This book is also fondly dedicated to the three great women in my life: my wonderful wife, Barbara, my daughter and cowriter, Christina, and my remarkable younger daughter, Catherine, all of whom help me find my own personal balance point in life.

BRIAN

CONTENTS

INTRODUCTION

Too Much to Do, Too Little Time

Everyone today has too much to do and too little time. You often feel overwhelmed with your duties, tasks, and responsibilities. The challenge for you is to simplify your life in such a way that you spend more time doing the things that are most important to you and less time doing those things that are not important at all.

The best news is that you have the power, right now, to live a life with no regrets, where you feel fully engaged in your relationships and everything you do. You can choose to live a life where each day holds meaning and purpose and brings you joy. You can live a life that is focused, positive, and completely in balance with the person you really are deep inside.

The desire for peace of mind and the idea of living a balanced life are central to your happiness and well-being. When you start to live your life in balance as the very best person you could possibly be, you will enjoy the happiness you deserve and experience harmony among all the elements that make up a successful life for you, as you define it.

Your Balance Point

We are all unique individuals with our own values, vision, purpose, and goals. Each one of us has a different way of achieving true balance. Each person experiences true balance when she is operating at her own unique *balance point*. It is from your balance point that you experience the highest level of clarity, commitment, strength, and confidence to pursue your ambitions, both personally and professionally.

The key to success in any area is, first, to start from the right place, and second, to know what steps you need to take to get where you want to go.

In karate, this starting point is the *ready stance*. In ballet, it's *first position*. In painting, you *prime your canvas*. In baking, you *set the oven*. Every area of life has a correct point from which to start.

Finding Your Balance Point

Your greatest need is to understand how to identify your balance point, move to it at will, and automatically return to it whenever you want. You need to establish your balance point before you can set and achieve the goals that are important to you and live a life that is harmonious and truly balanced.

True Balance

True balance is what you experience when everything in your life feels as if it is in perfect harmony. When you enjoy true balance, you feel clear and focused. You go through your day with courage and confidence. You know what you want to accomplish, and you take the necessary steps to accomplish it. Physically, you feel calm and relaxed. You have the health and energy to do whatever you choose to do.

Emotionally, you feel grounded and happy. You feel connected to others and appreciate your own unique self. Your mind, body, and spirit are in perfect alignment. You feel at one with the universe. This is your goal.

The Inner Experience

True balance is something you experience deep inside. It can be achieved only when you are confident with your choices. Once you have identified what enables you to enjoy this feeling of true balance, it is easier to find and easier to maintain.

You are experiencing true balance when you feel inspired and fully engaged in everything you do. Everything you choose to invest your time and energy into has special meaning for you. True balance is never threatened or influenced by the choices of others because it is a state of mind that is unique to each person. Your requirements for true balance will be exactly what you alone want and need.

False Balance

Generally speaking, people are impatient. They want whatever they want, and they want it now, even if they didn't know that they wanted it one minute ago. As a result, they gravitate readily to the quick fix of getting back into balance with as little effort as possible. They can easily be attracted to activities that will bring them a sense of false balance rather than doing those things that are necessary for them to achieve true balance.

In our society, we quickly turn to consumption to feel better. We drink too much, eat too much, and buy too many things we don't need in search of an *external* means to achieve some form of relief or balance. These false balance options are usually just Band-Aids. They don't really change anything in our lives, except temporarily.

If you take a yoga class, you are not going to suddenly become more flexible. The flexibility you desire will require many weeks and even months of steady work on yourself.

If you spend two weeks on an extreme diet, you may drop a few pounds, but you will seldom achieve your ideal weight. And whatever weight you lose, you will quickly put back on again as you revert to your previous lifestyle.

If you go on a vacation but spend the majority of your time distracted by work and e-mails, you are not going to come home feeling refreshed or reconnected to your loved ones.

Too many people are seeking a magic pill that will solve their problems and help them achieve their goals quickly and easily. We want quick solutions to problems that have taken years to develop, and this is simply not possible.

Beware of Easy Answers

As it happens, numerous experts, coaches, psychologists, and counselors claim that they can help you find peace of mind and balance. Unfortunately, many of their methods are flawed. They don't work for two major reasons. The first reason is that most of the solutions offered by so-called authorities offer only a quick fix. They don't solve the root problem that is causing your unhappiness and imbalance in the first place.

The second flaw in their ideas is that what brings balance in the life of one person will not necessarily work for another.

You are unique. There never has been and never will be anyone exactly like you. You have had a unique set of experiences, starting in early childhood, that has made you the person you are today. You have made different choices and decisions throughout your life, tried different things, made different mistakes, and gone in different directions from anyone else. The person you are today is a sum total result of thousands of small actions, thoughts, feelings, decisions, regrets, and events that, in combination, no one else has ever experienced.

Because you are special and unique, there are no pat answers or simple solutions that you can take out of a box or a book and apply directly to your life to solve your problems and achieve your goals.

Just as with most medicines, any advice or insight that you acquire may have side effects and cause unexpected reactions. You should always keep an open mind when you hear new ideas and then think about which parts of these ideas might apply directly to your own personal situation.

Falling Victim to False Balance

Many people are lured into the trap of false balance because they are unfocused and feel so overwhelmed with being out of balance that they don't even know where to start their quest. They feel as if they are spending their lives treading water and hoping not to sink. They are often stuck in a comfort zone, doing the same things in the same way, and disconnected from the reality of what a balanced life looks and feels like.

Often, they don't like and respect themselves. They lack the confidence to make tough choices and to take the actions necessary to align their lives with what they truly value.

They are unclear about what is important to them and what motivates them.

You often see this situation with people who look to others to determine how to achieve their own state of balance. They will compare themselves to someone else and emulate what they see in hopes of achieving what they perceive is balance and happiness. For example, a son who is unclear about his career choice decides to copy his father's choice of career in an attempt to gain his father's approval. He is unclear about what he wants personally, so he imitates his father because that choice is comfortable and safe. His attempt to achieve balance the way his father appears to have achieved his state of balance will result in the son's finding false balance because his career choice will not be a reflection of what he truly values.

When people are in a state of false balance, they feel disengaged and powerless to change the world around them. They often turn to buying things to feel better. They buy things they don't need, spend money they don't have, eat the wrong foods, and turn to alcohol and drugs to feel better. They are desperate to fill the hole inside them and regain some sense of clarity and control in their lives.

Clarity Is the Key to Finding Balance

When people do not feel in control of their lives, they lose focus and lack commitment. Instead of directing their own lives, they react and respond to the behaviors and opinions of others. They end up investing their time and energy in things that don't bring them joy.

For example, a woman who has two young children wants to start a business, but she keeps agreeing to take on volunteer projects at her children's school. As a result, she has no time to work on developing her business. She becomes overwhelmed with all her commitments and does not set aside any time to pursue her own ambitions. She feels out of control—or controlled by the people around her. This robs her of self-confidence. She feels frustrated and unhappy. She finds herself reacting to the needs of others because she is unclear about her own needs and her own direction.

Without clarity, you cannot design a plan, and without a clear plan, there is no way that you can know what specific actions to take and which direction to go. However, when you become clear about and committed to what is important to you, design a plan for your life, and ensure that your life on the outside becomes a reflection of your desired life on the inside, you will begin to operate from your balance point and begin to make tremendous progress in every area of your life.

For you to enjoy the kind of life you have imagined, and to achieve everything that is possible for you, you will probably have to make a series of positive and constructive changes to the way you think, feel, and react to the world around you. The good news is that at any time, you can resolve to make the rest of your life the best of your life. You can make a decision today to become everything you are capable of becoming. You can take complete control of your present and design your ideal future.

In this book, you will learn how to identify, achieve, and maintain your balance point. You will learn how to move smoothly and confidently through life, recognizing when you are out of balance and knowing exactly what you need to do to restore your balance point once more.

Clarifying Your Values

First, you will learn how to identify your values in life and become crystal clear about what is truly important to you. You will learn how to organize your life around your values. You will learn how to set boundaries and insist on living your life in alignment with your values, not compromising them at the request or demand of others.

In addition, you will learn how to create an exciting vision of your ideal life sometime in the future, as well as what you will need to do to make your perfect future life into your current reality.

You will also learn how to infuse your life with meaning and purpose and organize your activities so that you really make a difference in every part of your life.

Setting Goals and Being Proactive

You will learn how to set and achieve your goals and make sure that everything you do on the outside is in harmony with what is most important to you on the inside.

You will also learn to become proactive and choose where you invest your time and energy. Instead of reacting to the circumstances around you and spending your limited time and energy achieving the goals of others, you will focus your energies accomplishing what is most important to you.

Setting Priorities and Managing Your Time

You will learn how to take complete control over your time and your life, how to set priorities, and how to get more done, faster and more easily, than ever before. You will also learn that by setting priorities on your goals and activities, and managing your time effectively, you will both energize and simplify your life.

Operating from Your Balance Point

When you learn how to blend your values, vision, mission, purpose, goals, and priorities into a clear life plan that reflects all the aspects of your unique personality, you will be able to establish and operate from your own unique balance point.

When you operate from your own personal balance point, you will enjoy unshakable self-confidence and self-esteem. You will achieve complete balance between your personal and professional ambitions and know that you are making every day count. When you choose to live your life from your balance point—in harmony with your values, vision, purpose, goals, and priorities—you will be choosing to live a life with no regrets.

Our goal in writing this book is to give you the practical, proven steps that you can take immediately to clarify your priorities, simplify your life, and achieve all your hopes and dreams. Let's get started!

CHAPTER ONE

Determine Your Values and Start from the Right Place

In the pages ahead, you will learn how to discover who you really are; what values drive your beliefs, attitudes, and actions; and exactly what you need to do to create a plan that ensures a life of passion, purpose, and self-direction.

Clarity Is Essential

The starting point of designing a wonderful life is for you to develop absolute clarity about who you are and what matters to you. This means that you must be clear about your *values*. It seems that successful, happy people know what their values are and what they stand for, and they refuse to compromise them. Most of the great men and women of history have been admired because of their character, because of their adherence to a set of values that enabled them to overcome incredible adversity and go on to accomplish extraordinary things. And this can be true for you as well.

Everything happens for a reason. Success and happiness are not accidents. Failure and underachievement are not accidents either. There are definite reasons for everything that happens, and most of these reasons are contained within yourself.

Fortunately, you can control the things that you think, say, and do, and by controlling them, you can design the kind of life that you want and create the kind of future that is possible for you.

When you become clear about your values and what is truly important to you, it becomes easier to make a plan for your future. People who know what they want and are clear about what they are working toward feel engaged and inspired by their lives. Developing clarity about your values is the essential first step to creating a happy life. When you become clear about these values, you will start operating from your own personal balance point.

What Are Values?

Your values lie at the core of your character and your personality. Values are the foundation of your self-concept. They are like the axle around which your entire life turns. They are the primary drivers and motivators that push you forward. They determine who you are and who you are not, what matters to you and what does not.

You've heard the saying "life is a journey." Let's use that idea to help illustrate the role that values play in your life. On your life journey you will travel to many destinations. Just as you wouldn't just jump in your car and drive or hop on a plane and fly off somewhere, you wouldn't start without a clear destination. Your values largely determine which destination you choose. Do you prefer warm weather or cool weather? A city vacation or a seaside holiday? Luxury or budget? Are you interested in museums and other cultural experiences? The destination you choose and the trip you take will be a reflection of what is important to you, very much a reflection of your values. These values lie at the core of the person you really are inside, your self-concept.

Your Self-Concept

Your self-concept is your bundle of beliefs and ideas about yourself and your world. It is how you think and feel about yourself and every part of your life. It is the central or master program of your subconscious computer. Your self-concept precedes and predicts your performance and effectiveness in everything you do.

According to humanistic psychologist Carl Rogers, your self-concept is made up of three parts, like three overlapping spheres, each touching the other. These are your *ideal self*, your *self-image*, and your *self-esteem*. Let's look at each of them in order.

Your Ideal Self

Your *ideal self* is a combination of all the values and virtues that you admire in yourself and in others. It is a picture of the perfect person that you would like to be at some time in the future. Your ideal self is your vision of the very best person that you could possibly become.

Your Self-Image

Your *self-image* is the second part of your self-concept. This is the person you see on the inside and think of yourself as being. It is often called your "inner mirror"—you always behave on the outside the way you see yourself behaving on the inside.

You might identify yourself by your physicality, by the social roles you play, or by your personality traits. All improvements in your outer life begin with an improvement in how you think about yourself—your mental and physical self-image.

Your Self-Esteem

The third part of your self-concept, your *self-esteem*, is perhaps the most important part of your personality. This is the "reactor core" of your personality, the energy source and center that determines the power of your personality. Your level of self-esteem is the foundation of your *self-confidence*, the most important quality of all for success in a busy, competitive world.

Your self-esteem is defined as "how much you like yourself." The more you like yourself, or even *love yourself*, the better you do at anything that you attempt. And the better you do at your work and in other areas of your life, the more you like and respect yourself. Each aspect feeds the other: the more you like yourself, the better you do, and the better you do, the more you like yourself, in a continuing upward spiral of higher performance and higher self-esteem.

Your self-esteem is greatly affected by the relationship between your self-image and your ideal self. The more consistent the person you see yourself as being today is with your ideal self—the person you would like to be in the future—the higher will be your self-esteem.

The greater the distance between the person you see yourself as being today and the person you want most to be, the lower will be your self-esteem and self-confidence. When you are clear about your values and your ideals and you live every day in a manner that is consistent with those values, your self-image will move closer toward your ideal self, your self-esteem will increase, and you will feel a tremendous sense of self-respect and personal pride. This is our goal for you throughout this book.

The link between your self-image and your ideal self is why it is said that all problems in your personal life can be solved by a return to values, to the very best that is in you.

Select Your Values

What are your values? This is a great question! How do you determine what your values are today, and how do you decide what values are most important to you going forward?

There are two ways to determine your current values. The first is to look at your behaviors or actions on a day-to-day, hour-by-hour, and minute-to-minute basis. Your true values and beliefs are most often expressed in your *actions*. What you say or hope or wish or intend to do or be in the future does not really matter. Only your actions in the moment tell you, and everyone around you, what you truly value and who you really are deep inside.

The second way to assess your values is to look at how you behave under stress. When you are under stress or pressure and you are forced to choose one action or another, your choice will express your true values.

For example, ask yourself, "If I found out today that I had only six months to live, how would I spend my time?" Your answer to this question will tell you what is most important to you in life at this moment.

You can also determine what you truly value by looking at what makes you the happiest and what qualities you most respect and admire in others.

Clarifying your true values is not easy. Some people choose to attend intensive, three-day seminars on the subject of values clarification to help them develop absolute clarity about what is important to them in every area of life. These seminars are often life changing for the simple reason that most people, even highly educated and intelligent people, are unclear and unsure about what their values really are or what they should be.

But once you are clear about your values, and their order of priority in your life, and you resolve to live consistent with these values, you will feel a tremendous sense of liberation and exhilaration. Life will become simple and clear. You will know what to do and what not to do. Decision making will become easier. You will feel that you are becoming the very best person you can possibly be.

Let's talk now about three different kinds of values: character values, life category values, and values around roles and identities.

Character Values

Following is a list of character values, also referred to as "virtues." Virtues are the admirable and desirable qualities and strengths that make up a person's character. They are usually developed early in life as the result of parental influence and example. Virtues can also be developed in adulthood by repetition and practice and by refusing to allow exceptions.

Read through this list and ask yourself, "What kind of person am I?" Circle those words that you believe best describe your character and guide your choices and actions today, or jot them down on a piece of paper. Also circle or write down those virtues and values that you would most like to develop in the future. This combination constitutes your ideal self.

Accepting	Accountable	Assertive
Brave	Cautious	Committed
Compassionate	Confident	Considerate
Content	Cooperative	Courageous
Courteous	Creative	Curious
Defiant	Dependable	Determined
Devoted	Diligent	Disciplined
Discrete	Eloquent	Empathic
Enthusiastic	Faithful	Flexible
Focused	Forgiving	Friendly
Frugal	Generous	Gentle
Graceful	Grateful	Helpful
Honest	Humble	Humorous
Idealistic	Impartial	Industrious
Innocent	Joyful	Just
Kind	Knowledgeable	Liberal
Loving	Loyal	Moderate
Modest	Obedient	Open-minded
Optimistic	Orderly	Passionate
Patient	Peaceful	Persistent
Pious	Prudent	Punctual
Purposeful	Rational	Resourceful
Respectful	Responsible	Righteous
Selfless	Self-sacrificing	Servicing
Sensitive	Sincere	Spontaneous
Steadfast	Strong	Tactful
Tolerant	Trusting	Trustworthy
Truthful	Vital	Wise
Zealous		

Now, look at your selections and choose the one value that is most important to you. (This is not easy!) Continue through your selected values and decide which is your second most important value and then your third, fourth, and fifth. This is a great exercise and an excellent starting point.

Which are the most important values in your life today? (Write them here or on a piece of paper.)

1. _____

2. _____

3. _____

4. _____

5. _____

Identifying which values are most important to you, and their order of importance, helps you live a more successful, balanced life for three reasons. The first reason is that the values you admire and desire the most are unique and personal to you. To achieve balance in your life, you need to be clear and committed to what matters most to you.

The second reason is that the more your daily words and actions are consistent with your most deeply felt values, the higher will be your self-esteem and the more you will like and respect yourself. The more self-esteem you enjoy, the greater will be your self-confidence. The more self-confidence you have, the more energy and determination you will have to move forward and achieve your goals. Nothing will stop you.

The third reason why clarity regarding your values is essential is that to determine how to set goals and priorities, you need to know what you really want and care about more than anything else.

Life Category Values

We are shaped and motivated by the qualities of our character and the values we place on each different part, or category, of our lives. In achieving balance in our day-to-day lives, it is usually the life category values where we strive to achieve balance the most.

Before you can achieve success in your personal and professional lives, you must first determine what "success" looks like for yourself. Finding your balance point requires that you decide what is most important to you among these categories and then where and how you should invest your time and energy.

Look through the following list and circle the words or phrases that describe the most important elements of your life, both present and in the future, or write them down on a piece of paper. You may select all of them or only a few; there is no right answer—only what is right for you.

Romantic partnerships	Family
Children	Parents
Friends	Social life
Money	Work
Career	Home
Travel	Material things
Religion	Health
Fitness	Education
Spirituality	Community

Which are your five most important categories, those areas that take up, or that you wish would take up, most of your time?

1. _____

2. _____

3. _____

4. _____

5. _____

Does your life reflect all the categories you listed? Are there certain categories that are important to your happiness and fulfillment but to which you are not devoting enough time and energy?

You may find that you selected many of the categories, but not all of them are of the same importance to you. Later we will discuss how to prioritize your values and live a life that accurately reflects the significance you give each one. In addition, you will learn how to establish your values and priorities and how they may change in importance throughout your life.

Role and Identity Values

When asked to describe themselves, people often mention the roles they play and the jobs they do. Just as certain virtues are more meaningful to us than others, we also place different degrees of importance on our various identities and activities. Each person usually has multiple identities, each of which is more or less important than the others.

One person may value creative expression and identify strongly with being an *artist*. That same person may identify her role as a *professional* to be more central to her overall identity. She would therefore describe herself first as a professional and second as an artist. For many women, this is a particularly challenging exercise. Often, women who establish themselves in a career and then stop to raise a family find themselves struggling between their role as a professional and their role as a mother. For these women, determining how to divide their time is absolutely essential to establishing their personal balance point and to feeling happy and confident about how they spend their time.

As you go through the following exercise, be aware that a significant characteristic of values, especially our values around roles, is that they are constantly changing and evolving. At some points in your life you may identify more strongly with one role and then at a later point you may find yourself or imagine yourself connected to another. Circle or write down on a piece of paper the roles that you identify with and that are important to you now or that may be important sometime in your future.

Child	Mother	Father
Grandmother	Grandfather	Wife
Husband	Friend	Teacher
Student	Leader	Employer
Employee	Partner	Artist
Professional	Stepmother	Stepfather
Aunt	Uncle	Sister
Brother	Citizen	Devout follower

Of the roles you selected, which one do you identify with the most? Second most? Third? Fourth? Fifth? You can list roles relevant to your life right now or a combination of the roles you play now and the roles you hope to play in the future.

1. _____

2. _____

3. _____

4. _____

5. _____

Becoming clear about what drives you, what you value, and how you prioritize those values is essential to creating your personal life design and learning how to operate from your balance point. Without crystal clear awareness of what truly matters to you, your path will be unclear, your foundation will not feel solid, and you will never experience the true balance and harmony that is possible for you.

Once you take the time to think about the values discussed in this chapter and acknowledge how integral they are to your overall sense of happiness, you will probably want to change the way you live your life and get yourself back on track. You will see clearly what you need to change to begin operating from your own balance point. This clarity will enable you to feel more empowered to become the kind of person who can achieve any goal you set for yourself.

Prioritizing Your Values

You need to be clear about your values if you want to live a happy life. You must also be clear about the priority in which you organize your values. Which value is *most* important to you? Which value is *second* most important to you? Which value is *third*, and so on? This order of priority largely determines the structure of your personality—what you think and feel, what you say, and what you do—especially when you are forced to choose between one value and another.

Imagine that you know two people, one person who values *security* above all else and another person who values *opportunity* or new experiences above all else. Here's the question: Would there be a difference between these two people in terms of their character and personality? Would the difference be small or large? The answer is that the difference would be *enormous*. The two people would be completely different from each other in their beliefs, expectations, attitudes, and behaviors.

Two Examples

Imagine two men: one is a lawyer and the other is a salesman. The lawyer goes to work early in the morning and comes home late at night. He often has to work on projects during the weekend and has little extra time to spend with his two young sons. However, he loves his job and feels fully engaged at work. He feels proud of his accomplishments and knows that he is providing well for his family.

The salesman travels extensively for work and is often away from home several days at a time. When he is home, he divides his time between his family and professional projects he is working on. He too places tremendous value on his ability to provide for his family.

Both men highly value their careers, take pride in their achievements, and feel good about their accomplishments.

You may think that because both of these men spend the majority of their time working, their lives are out of balance. But the reality is that these men both enjoy their work and highly value their ability to provide for their families. They are actually living their lives in alignment with their highest values and are therefore in balance.

No two people operate from the same balance point. People are different and contribute in unique ways to society. No two are exactly the same.

Learning to operate from your balance point requires that you stop comparing yourself to others and start to appreciate the differences that exist among people. What is right for you and what is right for someone else do not have to be the same. When you are clear about your own personal values and you decide to live by them, without compromise, you can feel calm and confident no matter what others do or say. You can then find and maintain your own balance point.

ACTION EXERCISES

1. Every day for a week, ask yourself, "What do I value the very most in life?" Your first answers to this question may be automatic but not necessarily accurate. Keep asking, and let your thoughts go where they lead you. You may be surprised at your final answer.

2. Imagine that you could have two words inscribed on your tombstone to summarize the kind of person you became in your lifetime. What two virtues or qualities would you want inscribed after the words, "Here lies (you). He/She was (two qualities)."?

CHAPTER TWO

Discover What Holds You Back

Your values lie at the core of your personality, as we have said before. When you are living in harmony with your values, you can tell because you experience peace of mind, calmness, and even joy. When you are out of balance and off track, you feel the opposite. Negative emotions, unhappiness, and discontent of any kind are nature's way of telling you to return to your values. You can almost immediately restore your feelings of peace and happiness by returning to what is really important to you and then by refusing to compromise your values.

Everyone has had the experience of being in a stressful situation, an unhappy relationship, or a bad job. You knew deep inside that something wasn't right. The worse the situation became, the more you felt forced to compromise your values instead of doing what you knew was right for you and insisting on your own happiness and well-being. The longer you stayed in that bad situation, the more stressed, unhappy, and actually detached from life and other people you became.

Finally, however, you took a deep breath, mustered up your courage, and decided to "do the right thing." You walked away from the bad job, even though you didn't know what you were going to do and even though you had bills to pay. You walked away from the bad relationship, even though you had no idea how you might ever find another, better relationship.

And then something absolutely terrific happened! You felt *exhilarated*. You felt wonderful. You felt happy and relieved. You felt as though a great burden had been lifted off your shoulders. You felt truly happy and almost laughed out loud as you walked away.

Why was this? The answer is simple. Whenever you decide to return to your values and get back on track, nature rewards you by giving you a feeling of joy and happiness. The purpose of this joyous feeling is to encourage you to live your life by your values more often.

The Obstacles to Happiness

There is no question that your values are central to your life and to everything that happens to you. Living by your values is absolutely essential for success, self-esteem, happiness, and peace of mind. Every time that you deviate from or compromise your core beliefs and values, you feel uncomfortable, unhappy, stressed, and anxious and you suffer low self-esteem. You don't like and respect yourself as much. This is why we say that almost all problems in your personal life can be solved by a return to your values.

Why is it then that people get off track and compromise their values, leading to frustration, failure, unhappiness, and feelings of inferiority and worthlessness? There are several reasons, all mental and emotional. Fortunately, you can identify them and remove these obstacles from your pathway toward becoming the best person you could possibly be.

1. *People feel a sense of undeservingness.* This is one of the main obstacles to happiness in adult life. Many people feel that they do not deserve to be happy, to be popular, to be successful, and to be loved and respected by others. They do not feel that they deserve to be successful, healthy, and wealthy and to live wonderful, exciting lives.

2. *People are unclear about their values.* They have never taken the time to sit down and think through what is truly important to them, what they care about, and what takes priority over everything else in their lives. The minute they do and they begin to establish a path for their lives with clear direction, they suddenly feel happy and in control of their lives. They are no longer reacting to those around them. Instead, they are proactive. They make their own choices and decisions. Clarity is essential.

3. *People are so overwhelmed with the feeling of being unfocused and out of balance that they don't know where to start.* They are stuck in a comfort zone and disconnected from the reality of what a balanced life looks and feels like. As a result, their feeling of busyness, having no time for what's essential, causes them to make

thoughtless and impulsive choices. They are often en-
ticed by short-term pleasures and satisfactions that
tempt them to compromise their values for a quick fix.

4. *People don't consider the long-term consequences of their
   behaviors.* Short-term thinking is a major source of unhappiness, failure, and frustration in life.

   The most successful and happy people practice
   long-term thinking. They project themselves forward
   into the future and become clear about where they
   want to be five and ten years from today. They then
   evaluate each behavior in the short term with regard to
   what they really want to achieve in the long term.

   Developing a long-term vision of your ideal future
   dramatically improves the quality of your current decision making. The very act of taking a little time to
   think before you decide and act, and to be sure that
   your actions are consistent with the highest values to
   which you aspire, can improve your life dramatically.

5. *People desire the approval of others, and they feel that
   only by compromising their values will other people like
   them, respect them, hire them, promote them, pay them,
   or include them.* This desire can dominate the thinking, feelings, and behavior of adult individuals. They
   can become preoccupied with earning the approval
   of others and especially avoiding their criticism or
   disapproval.

   Because the approval of the important people in
   your life, especially your boss or spouse, is closely as-
   sociated with your feelings of security, and security is
   a key driving emotional factor, you can easily compromise your values in the search for this approval. But

the truth is that the only person whose approval you need is your own.

Put Your Own Happiness First

The most respected people in every society are those who clearly and distinctively express their own unique personalities. They are sure and unequivocal about their values and beliefs, and they refuse to compromise them for anyone or anything.

Ayn Rand was famous for pointing out that the achievement of your own happiness should be your highest value or goal in life. She said that you can determine how successful you are by how happy you feel about yourself minute by minute and hour by hour. Your personal happiness should be the barometer by which you judge your actions and your behaviors and especially your values.

There is some confusion on this point. People are taught that seeking their own happiness is somehow selfish. We are supposed to seek to make others happy first. But the truth is that you cannot give away what you do not have. You cannot make someone else happy unless you are happy yourself. If you truly want to make others happy, become a truly happy person. There is no other way.

When you are clear about your values, goals, and priorities, you operate from your balance point. As a result, you feel happy, clear, and focused. You go through your day with courage and confidence.

Values, Authenticity, and Balance

You must choose to be true to at least one person: *yourself*. Having integrity and being authentic is the only way to succeed at establishing and operating from your balance point. As Shakespeare wrote, "To thine own self be true, and it must follow, as the night the day, thou canst not then be false to any man."

Remember that your balance point is completely unique to you. You may find that you share values with others and connect and relate with them based on those values, but you will also encounter many differences. Your goal is to find what is right for you and then have the strength and confidence to move through your life committed to living your own personal set of values.

Don't feel threatened or doubt your values based on comparing yourself to others. You need to do what is right for you and embrace the idea that other people are doing what is right for them. Remember, "Different strokes for different folks."

Three Sets of Values

Imagine three women. The first woman decided that she wanted to get married and have children right after college. She chose to build her career after her children were all in school. The second woman decided to establish her career after college and spent ten years working hard to build a solid reputation and achieve success in her chosen profession. Only then did she decide to have children. The third woman decided to do both—to build her career while also getting married and raising children. All three women shared the values of having a career and being a mother, but each of them pursued those goals in her own unique way. Each of the three ways was a reflection of one woman's values and the unique balance point that she had.

Decide today to live a wonderful life. Carefully examine each of the obstacles to happiness—the reasons that people give for compromising their true values and settling for less than they are really capable of.

Remember that each of these obstacles exists only in your mind, in your thinking. At any time, you can throw off your self-limiting ideas and become a fully functioning, fully mature, happy person. You can discard your limitations and liberate yourself to realize your full potential. You can determine your own balance point, your own set of values and goals, and return to it whenever you want.

~~~~~~~**ACTION EXERCISES**~~~~~~~

1. Select one self-limiting belief that might be holding you back from achieving the happiness and joy you deserve, and ask yourself, "What if this belief were not true; what would I do then?"

   Whatever your answer, act as if it were impossible to fail, and it shall be.

2. Imagine that you have no limitations on what you can be, do, or have in any area of your life. Imagine that you had all the money and resources, talent and ability, knowledge and experience, and people and contacts that you require to achieve anything you really want. What is the first thing you would do differently in your life and relationships?

CHAPTER THREE

Create Your Vision and Be Powered by Clarity

You have now determined your values and know what you stand for and believe in. You have identified some of the false ideas that might be holding you back. It is now time for you to start designing your life plan and determine your *vision* for yourself, your perfect life in every respect. If your life were ideal, what would it look like? How would it be different from your life as it is today?

Your ability to create a clear, exciting vision of your perfect life at some time in the future is your starting point as you begin to operate from your balance point. The vision of your ideal life is the target you are aiming at. For you to feel engaged and present every day, you need to focus all your actions, time, and energy on that target. In other words, to succeed in your personal and professional ambitions and do so while experiencing that feeling of true balance, you have to be clear about what your target is.

Imagine No Limitations

Again, start by imagining that you have no limitations at all. Imagine that you could be, do, or have anything in the world that you really want.

The key question is, What do you *really, really, really* want to do with your life?

Imagine that you have a magic wand and that you could wave it over any part of your life and make it perfect in every way. How would it be different from the way it is today?

Your Thoughts Become Your Realities

Perhaps the greatest discovery in human history is that you become what you think about most of the time.

What do you think about most of the time? The Law of Correspondence says, "Your outer world will tend to be a reflection of your inner world." This law tends to be true in all areas, from the things you want to acquire or achieve to your fundamental beliefs about yourself and others.

What you think about most of the time triggers your *reticular activating system*, causing you to become more aware of things in your environment. For example, if you decide you want to buy a red car, you will start seeing red cars everywhere. If you believe people are basically friendly with good intentions, the people around you will appear friendly and good-natured.

It Goes Both Ways

Unfortunately, what you think about is a two-edged sword. If you believe people are unfriendly and untrustworthy, you will see examples of this everywhere. Your experience of the world outside yourself will be directly affected by your beliefs and the way you see the world on the inside. You've heard it said that "You don't believe what you see; you see what you already believe." What you believe is a reflection of who you are, your innermost convictions about yourself and the world around you.

Everything you see in your outer world reflects back to you something that is going on inside you, something that matters to you. To live an extraordinary life, you must develop a clear, exciting picture of what your ideal life would be like in every detail. Once you become clear about what you want, some amazing power in the universe will begin to create this life in the world around you. You will start to attract people and resources to make your dreams into realities. Opportunities will begin to emerge to help you achieve your ideal life exactly as you have designed it.

This does not mean that if you imagine your ideal life, it will magically appear without any effort from you. But you can begin to achieve your ideal life only when you have determined what it looks like. You can't hit a target that you can't see.

Remember that life is a journey. It is up to you to determine what kind of trip you are going to take. You are free to visualize the perfect destination for your life and then determine *how* to get there.

The Magic Question

Can you guess what happy, successful people think about most of the time? The answer is both simple and amazing. Top people think about what they *want*, and *how* to get it, most of the time. They think about accomplishing and enjoying their goals, dreams, and ambitions most of the time. They are constantly asking the magic question *how*.

How is the question of the leader, the optimist, the builder, the mover and shaker. Whenever you ask the question *how*, you trigger ideas for actions that you can take to move ahead faster in life in every area.

The top 10 percent of people think about the *future* most of the time. They think about where they are going and what they want most of the time. They face all kinds of obstacles and confidently navigate around them. They think about the actions they can take each day to move themselves in the direction of their hopes and dreams. They only ask *how*.

Become a Leader

You are the leader of your life. You are responsible for creating your own future. Only you can do this; no one else can.

The mark of future-oriented people is that they continually practice *idealization* regarding their lives and their future. They project themselves forward and imagine that their future is perfect in every way. They then come back to the present and decide what they will have to do, starting today, to create the future that they desire. And you can do this as well.

First, you need to develop clarity in four key areas about who you are, what is truly important to you, and what you want to achieve in the future.

One: Your Professional Identity— Developing Your Business

If you have a business, the starting point in strategic planning is for you to develop a clear picture, in writing, of what you want your business to look like at some time in the future. What kinds of products and services do you want to produce? Who are your customers? What levels of sales and profitability do you want to achieve? What kind of reputation do you want to enjoy? What kind of people do you want to have working in your business, and how can you attract them?

Begin by projecting yourself forward five years. Create a *five-year fantasy*, and imagine that your business was perfect in every way five years from today. Think on paper. Write down every word you can think of to describe your perfect business at some time in the future.

Many of our clients have doubled, tripled, and increased the sales and profitability of their businesses as a result of conducting this exercise. When you become very clear about your ideal future vision for your business, you will begin to see immediately what you should start doing and stop doing. By comparing your current activities with your future ideal, you can develop clear ideas about what you should be doing more of or less of to make that ideal come true.

Imagine Your Perfect Career

You can conduct this same exercise for your career and your income. Project yourself forward five years. What would you like to be doing in five years, and whom would you like to be doing it with? How much would you like to be earning year by year? If your job, career, and income were perfect in every way, what would they look like? And most

39

importantly, how would they be different from the way they are today?

Sometimes people get stuck on this and struggle to identify their ideal job. One way to become clear about this is to think about the activities that you enjoy most at work. What special skills do you have or desire to acquire? Can you think of a way to apply your special talents to your work or to develop some kind of product or service that would integrate your passion, skills, and experience to create your ideal job?

To achieve something that you have never achieved before, you are going to have to do something you've never done before. To create your ideal career, you may have to step outside your comfort zone. You may have to learn and apply skills that you've never had before. You may have to learn to think differently about yourself and your potential in your career.

Describe It in Detail

Make a list of everything you would have to do, starting today, to create your vision of the perfect career for you. Practice "back from the future" thinking. Project yourself forward five years and then look back to the present day. What would have to happen to get you from where you are today to where you want to be in the future?

Two: Your Family and Personal Relationships

The second area where you need to create an ideal future picture has to do with your family and relationships. Fully 85 percent of your happiness will be determined by having the right people in your life. Unfortunately, fully 85 percent of your unhappiness will be caused by having the wrong people in your life as well, both in the past and in the present.

Wave your magic wand again. Project yourself forward three to five years and imagine that your family life and relationships were perfect in every way. What would they look like?

Whom would you be with if your relationships were perfect in every way? Whom would you *no longer* be with? What kind of partnership would you have? If you imagine an ideal family, what kind of lifestyle would you have? Would you have children? If so, what kind of mother or father would you be? What kind of home would you live in? What kind of activities would you engage in during your leisure time? What sort of life would you want to create for the members of your family?

These questions are too important to be left to chance. Too many people go passively through life, accepting whatever happens to them. They settle for far less than is truly possible.

But this is not for you. Your job is to imagine that you have no limitations. You have all the knowledge and all the skills you need, or you can acquire them. You have all the time and money that you need, or you can get them in the future. You have all the friends and contacts. You have all the education and experience. Imagine you have no limits on what you can accomplish. But you must be clear about your ideal future.

Three: Your Health

The third area for you to idealize is your health and fitness. Project yourself forward three to five years and imagine that you enjoy superb physical health, energy, and fitness. Your body feels good and you are free of pain and illness. You sleep soundly and have ample energy to be active and focused all day long. You are able to pursue physical activities that you enjoy. Your body is strong and dependable. You feel wonderful about yourself most of the time.

What does that future look like for you? How would your ideal body feel to you? How much would you weigh? How much sleep would you get each night? What physical activities would you engage in on a regular basis? How would you maintain balance in your body? Would you get regular massages? Would you stretch or do yoga? Would you meditate daily? How would you describe your ideal health and fitness?

What sorts of foods would you eat and how much of them? What foods would you no longer eat? What changes would you make in your health habits?

Now come back to the present. How would that future ideal be different from your reality today? What would have to happen, starting right now, for you to create your image of a balanced, healthy body?

Four: Your Money and Investments

The fourth area for idealization has to do with your financial situation, especially your long-term dream of financial freedom and financial independence.

It is normal, natural, and healthy for you to want to reach the point where you have enough money so that you never have to worry about money again. In fact, the Bible does not say that money is the root of all evil. It says, "Love of money is the root of all evil."

In fact, *lack of money* is probably the root of most evils in our society. Lack of money is the major reason for the failure of businesses and organizations. It is the major cause of arguments that lead to separation and divorce. It is a major source of stress and psychosomatic illness (*psycho*, the mind, makes *soma*, the body, ill) that can lead to strokes, heart attacks, cancer, and even suicide. Lack of money is not a good thing.

Project yourself forward five years. Again, practice "back from the future" thinking. If your financial life were ideal at some time in the future, what would it look like? And how would it be different from the way it is today?

Design Your Perfect Financial Life

You can either live by *accident* or live by *design*. You can either be proactive and take action or be reactive to circumstances. The majority of people live by accident, passively accepting whatever happens to them, as though they had little or no control over their financial lives. But when you live by design, you make a clear decision that you are going to get out of debt and achieve financial independence in a specific period of time and by using specific plans and strategies.

How much money would you like to have invested and working for you? How much money would you like to be earning from your savings and investments each month and each year? How much money would you have to earn and accumulate to get out of debt and to achieve financial independence?

Once you are clear about your future vision of your financial life, come back to the present and ask, "What would have to happen for me to achieve this ideal? What is the first step that I could take, starting today, to make my financial life ideal at some time in the future?"

Take the First Step

Most important of all, what is the first step that you should take to begin creating your desired future? All of success begins with your taking the first step. As Confucius said, "A journey of a thousand leagues begins with a single step." What is yours?

Take that first step. And when you do, you will see the second step. When you take the second step, the third step will appear. You will always be able to see one step ahead. You can accomplish any goal that you set for yourself if you just take it one step at a time.

Believe in Yourself

Perhaps the most negative words you can use are "I can't!"

It is amazing how many people dismiss their hopes and dreams by simply saying "I can't." They then think about all the reasons why something they want is not possible for them. Saying "I can't" is like slamming on the brakes of your own potential. Those words paralyze you and block you from taking action. They hold you back unnecessarily.

The way that you can overcome the fear of failure, characterized by the words "I can't," is by neutralizing that feeling with the magical words "I can do it!"

Whenever you think of anything that you really, really, really want, immediately affirm, "I can do it! I can do anything that I put my mind to! I can accomplish any goal that I set if I am willing to work at it long enough and hard enough."

When you repeat to yourself, "I can do it! I can do it! I can do it!" over and over, you will eventually program your subconscious mind in such a way that you become *unstoppable*.

You will develop incredible reserves of persistence and determination. No matter what obstacles appear, you will find a way to go over them, around them, or through them. Nothing will stop you.

Resist the Phrase "I'll try"

The words "I'll try," are simply an excuse for failing—in advance. When a person says, "I will try to do it for you by Thursday" they are signaling to you quite clearly that, "I am going to fail. I am not going to do it by Thursday. This is the way I let you know, by using the words 'I'll try.'"

Instead of saying, "I'll try," you should say "I will do it. I will do a specific thing by a specific date."

No excuses. No blaming. No rationales for failure to do what you said you would do. Instead, say "I can do it! I can do it! I can do it!"

The Power of Visualization

You can apply the exercise of idealization in every area of your life. Painters dream of painting. Writers dream of writing. Adventurous people dream of travelling. Some people dream of becoming more involved and making a greater contribution to their church or their country. Others dream of mastering new subjects or new skills.

Your ability to visualize, to imagine, to create exciting pictures of your ideal future life is one of the greatest powers that you have. With the proper use of visualization, you can step on the accelerator of your own potential. You can accomplish vastly more than you ever dreamed possible in designing and creating your ideal life.

Three Essential Qualities

There are three important qualities you need in visualization and in the achievement of any goal that you set for yourself. They are *clarity*, *focus*, and *concentration*.

The development of clarity requires that you become absolutely certain about what you want and what your life will look like at some time in the future. You then focus your energies, without diversion or distraction, on doing exactly those things that move you toward the creation of your perfect life.

Finally, you concentrate single-mindedly on the most important things that you can do each day to enable you to fulfill your most exciting future vision.

Eliminate the Negatives

The greatest accelerator of happiness and achievement is optimism and positive thinking. The greatest detractor from happiness and achievement is pessimism and negative emotions. Your goal should be to have more of the former and less of the latter.

It Is Not What Happens to You

Shakespeare wrote, "There is nothing either good or bad, but *thinking* makes it so." What he meant is that it is not what happens to you but how you *interpret* what happens to you that determines whether you view it as a positive or a negative experience.

Dr. Martin Seligman of the University of Pennsylvania called this your "explanatory style." What he discovered in twenty-two years of research was that happy, successful people interpret each experience, even negative experiences, in a positive way. No matter what happens, they find something good in the experience. They focus on how they can learn and benefit.

It turns out that leaders never use the word "failure." As far as they are concerned, they never fail. They instead use expressions such as "learning experience." Sometimes they will use terms such as "expensive learning experience" or "painful learning experience," but they never use the word "failure" because they do not believe in failure.

The Thomas Edison Philosophy

One well-known story about Thomas Edison says that after more than five thousand experiments to develop the incandescent lightbulb, he was approached by a journalist who asked him why he persisted in the face of so many failures.

Edison answered with these wonderful words: "I have not failed; I've just found five thousand ways that will not work. This just puts me five thousand ways closer to the electric lightbulb. And I will find the right way sooner or later."

He went on to say, "When I decide to invent something, I begin with the belief that all I need to do is to identify and remove all the ways that won't work. Then, all that will be left is the one way that does work."

Bounce Back from Failure

It is the same in your life. As Nelson Mandela said, "We should all bear in mind that the greatest glory of living lies not in never falling but in rising every time you fall."

Here is a metaphor for you. Imagine that you have two fires. The first is the fire of *desire*: your hopes and dreams, ambitions, and images for the future. The second is the fire of *regret*: previous negative experiences that still make you unhappy when you think about them.

Each day you approach the fires with an armful of firewood. You can put your fuel on either fire. But what if you put all your fuel, your mental and emotional energy, on the fire of desire, keeping your hopes and dreams burning brightly in your mind all day long?

What happens to the other fire? Naturally, if you starve the other fire of fuel, it eventually goes out.

This is one of the most powerful of all principles for personal success and happiness. Resolve today to put all your mental energy on the fire of desire. Refuse to think or talk about things that happened in the past that still make you unhappy. The more time you spend thinking about what you want and how to achieve it, the more the old unhappy experiences will simply die out and have no more control over you.

Imagine the Possibilities

Helen Keller said, "The only thing worse than being blind is having sight but no vision."

You have the ability right now to visualize and create a wonderful future for yourself. Start by becoming clear about your values—what you stand for and believe in. Then create a fascinating vision of your perfect life, organized around your values and in harmony with them. Create exciting pictures of your dreams and aspirations as if they were already a reality. Then play and replay these pictures continually on the screen of your mind throughout the day and before you go to sleep. Develop the vividness and intensity of your mental pictures. Then practice seeing them with greater frequency and duration.

In so doing, you will activate all your mental powers, as well as the Law of Attraction, attracting into your life people and circumstances that will make your dreams come true. You will also activate the Law of Correspondence, causing your outer world to become a mirror image of the pictures that you hold in your mind most of the time. You will take complete control of your life and your destiny, and you will make your life into something wonderful. You will be operating at your balance point.

ACTION EXERCISES

1. Identify one major difference that would exist in your life if your business, career, or financial situation were ideal in every way. What would be the first step you could take to make this a reality?

2. Do the same with your family and personal relationships. If they were perfect in every way, how would they be different from your relationships today, and what one action could you take immediately to make this come true?

CHAPTER FOUR

Contribute with Purpose

At this point, you are clear about your values—
what you believe in and care about at a deep
level.

You now know the major obstacles to happiness.

You are also clear about your ideal vision—
your perfect life at some time in the future.

Now it is time for you to answer the question
why.

Why are you here? What gives your life meaning? Why do you do what you are doing rather
than a thousand other things? What would have
to happen for you to feel completely engaged and
truly balanced? What really matters to you?

Your Reason for Existence

Mark Twain once wrote, "The two most
important days in your life are the day
you are born and the day you find out
why."

Friedrich Nietzsche wrote, "He who has a *why* to live can bear almost any *how*."

Viktor Frankl, in his book *Man's Search for Meaning*, said that the most powerful desire of the human being is for a sense of meaning and purpose in life.

Albert Einstein was once asked, "What is the purpose of human life?" He thought for a while and then replied, "Only a life lived for others is the life worth while."

Exactly! We are here to serve others in some way. This is the primary source of meaning and purpose in our lives— service to others. We want to make a difference in the lives of other people.

It turns out that one of the requirements for self-esteem, self-respect, and personal pride is the deep-down feeling that you are making a contribution to others that is greater than what you are receiving from them. You feel that you are putting in more than you are taking out. What you do really matters to someone.

Deserving Our Lives

The fact is that we all make our livings and our lives by serving other people or something greater than ourselves in some way. Human beings are uniquely designed in such a way that we feel happy only when we are contributing, when we are somehow enriching the lives of others.

People who are not making a contribution, who are not serving anyone, who are taking without giving, are never happy. They suffer from low self-esteem and limited self-respect. They become resentful and jealous of those people who are busy and productive and who are making a differ-ence of some kind. Each person craves connection to others. Creating something that helps people or providing a service of some kind is one of the best ways to feel connected to something bigger than yourself. How you decide to serve others is one of the most important decisions you can ever make.

Contribute with Purpose—Your Perfect Job

A job is an opportunity to serve, more than anything else. Not only does it provide a way to satisfy your financial needs, but when your job holds meaning to you, your emotional and spiritual needs will be met as well.

Some of the happiest and most productive people are those who love their work, enjoy their coworkers, and feel that what they are doing benefits and serves others in some way. They believe they are making a difference.

Imagine your ideal job. If you could be successful at any job at all, what would you choose to do? If you could select any job in our society, what would it be?

If you had $20 million in the bank and only ten years to live and you had to work at something, what would you want to do? What work would you choose?

Deciding upon your ideal work is one of the great responsibilities of adult life. It is very much up to you. No one else can decide for you.

Look into Yourself

How can you find what it is that you love to do, what you are meant to do, the ideal work for which you were designed by nature?

You were born with special talents and abilities that make you different from anyone else who has ever lived. As Wayne Dyer once said, "Each child comes into this world with secret orders."

Michael Jordan said, "Everyone has talent, but *ability* takes hard work." Even if you have natural ability in some areas, it may take many years of hard work for you to develop to your full potential.

The Right Work for You

Following is a list of seven indicators of the right work for you, the career where you will feel fully engaged and where you will be the happiest in serving other people.

1. The right work for you is something that you really enjoy doing, something that you love to do.

2. The right work for you is easy for you to learn and easy to do. In many cases, you learned it automatically, without thought or effort.

3. You love learning more and more about the work if it is the right work for you.

4. When you are engrossed in this work, the hours fly past. You forget what time it is, and later you are surprised to see how much time has passed.

5. The right work for you gives you energy when you are doing it. You can spend hours at this work, often forgetting to eat.

6. If it is the right work for you, you want to be excellent at it, and you are constantly striving to learn and improve in that area.

7. If it is the right work for you, you admire the top people in your field, the ones who are recognized as excellent, and you want to be around them and learn from them.

Think back to a time when you experienced some of these indicators. In what areas of your life were you the happiest and most fulfilled? What were you doing when you were totally engrossed in your work or activities? What has been most responsible for your success in your work or career to date? Did the feeling of satisfaction and contentment come from a paid job or something in your personal life?

Work to Live or Live to Work?

In keeping with the theme of balance and operating from your balance point, understanding the distinction between working to live and living to work is very important. Some people feel fully invested and totally engaged in their professional roles and paid jobs. They are most confident, happy, and energized when they are working. However, some people are very good at their paid jobs, but they find that they feel most engaged, confident, and happy in their lives outside of their jobs.

For people who find their work to be fully satisfying, it would make sense to say that they would be operating from their unique balance point when they are investing most of their time and energy in their work. On the flip side, those people who feel more fully engaged in their personal lives would be operating from their balance point when most of their time and energy is focused on areas other than their paid jobs.

You can achieve balance and feel fully engaged in both your personal and professional roles when you organize your life around your values. Then, you can determine where your contributions will have the most meaning for you and those you serve.

The Clock Test

Here is a way you can tell if you are in the right job and contributing in the right place. It is called the "clock test."

What does the clock *mean* to you? For people in the *wrong* jobs or those who don't feel inspired by their work, the clock is a stern taskmaster. It tells them when they must start work, or resume working, and when they can quit their work for the day. They resent the clock and often feel that the clock has stopped.

These people feel disengaged from their work and are easily distracted by a variety of factors. They arrive at the last minute and leave at the first chance they get. Their job is not a source of fulfillment, and they do not feel satisfied at their work.

For people in the *right* jobs for them, the people who feel energized by their work, the clock is a competitor that they race against. The clock tells them how much time they have left before they will have to stop doing the work they enjoy. They are always trying to get more work done in the time allotted to them.

Success Leaves Tracks

When you are doing the work that you are designed to do, you will be eager to learn, to study, to take courses, to improve—evenings, weekends, and whenever you have any spare time.

However, if you have no desire to learn and improve, your current job may be the wrong one for you. This does not mean that it is a bad job. It simply means that the person you are, the values you embrace, and the requirements of the job do not fit together comfortably. When we talk about being out of balance and falling off track, a great indicator that your life is out of balance is your not feeling engaged and inspired in any area of your life, especially your work.

What if you do not feel inspired by your work? You may be quite good at the job that you do and feel confident in your professional contributions, but your job may be not a source of joy and inspiration. When you consider what contributions hold the most meaning for you, the answer may be something you do outside of your paid job.

Contribute with Purpose—Family, Friends, Community

You can serve in many other areas of life where you can enjoy profound feelings of meaning and purpose that are not work related. In fact, most people desire to both contribute professionally and contribute to their families.

Historically, women were responsible for rearing the children and maintaining the home. Men were expected to financially support their families with their jobs. However, there has been a major shift over time, and things have changed considerably. Now many more women are supporting their families financially, and many more men are caring for the children and maintaining the home.

Raise Happy Children

Most parents find great satisfaction and meaning in raising children. It is perhaps one of the most important jobs in our society. When you choose to become a parent, you can decide what kind of mother or father you want to be, based on your values.

Women especially struggle with this question. Most women want to both have a satisfying career and also be happy, successful mothers. But everyone is different. Some women are fully involved in their careers and find great meaning in their professional ambitions. Other women choose to dedicate all their time and energy to raising children. Some men choose to put their whole hearts into their work during the week and then are fully committed to their families on the weekend. There are many ways for men and women to achieve the balance they seek.

Raising children, for mothers and fathers, is a profound form of service. Most parents consider "serving" their children one of the most joyous and satisfying activities of life.

Choose Where to Serve

Many people serve in churches, nonprofits, government, and other organizations and receive profound mental and emotional benefits from this form of activity. Being a part of a community, organization, or cause brings feelings of satisfaction and personal worth. Service to others gives one a strong sense of being connected to something bigger than oneself.

How you choose to serve others, in whatever capacity, is not as important as the attitude and spirit that you bring to your service. As long as your basic motives in serving are to enrich and enhance the lives of your customers, your clients, your patients, or your recipients or beneficiaries and serving these people gives you joy and satisfaction, you are doing the right thing for you. Your life will feel meaningful and balanced.

Look into Yourself

What gives you your greatest feelings of meaning and purpose in life? What do you love doing? Who are the people you care about, respect, and want deeply to serve?

How could you organize your life so that you are serving more and more of these people better and better?

Finding the answers to these questions is the key to happiness, personal fulfillment, and true balance.

~~~~~~~~ **ACTION EXERCISES** ~~~~~~~~

1. Identify the kind of work you most enjoy and would want to do even if you weren't getting paid for it. What actions could you take, starting today, to do more of this work and get better at it?

2. Identify the people, causes, and organizations that you feel most strongly about and where you would like to serve and make a difference. What one action could you take immediately to become more involved in one of these areas?

CHAPTER FIVE

Set and Achieve All Your Goals

You have now thought through your values and determined what is most important to you in life. You have clarified your vision of what you would like to be, have, or do, based on your values. You have decided what gives meaning and purpose to your life, based on your sense of purpose and your vision. Now it is time for you to set clear, specific goals for your life and your future.

Your life begins to become a great life only when you clearly identify what it is that you want, make a plan to achieve it, and then work on that plan every single day.

The Goals Study

We heard about a study done with graduating seniors in 1979. The seniors were surveyed and asked if they had written goals and plans for their lives upon graduation. It turned out that only 3 percent of the graduating students had written goals and plans. Thirteen percent had goals, but they were not in writing. The other 84 percent had no goals or plans at all.

In 1989, ten years later, the researchers interviewed the members of that class again. They discovered that the 13 percent of students who had goals that were not in writing were earning, on average, *twice* as much as the 84 percent of students without goals. But the 3 percent of students who had written goals and plans—the top 3 percent—were earning, on average, *ten times* as much as the average of the other 97 percent.

There was no other correlation. The graduates had gone into different businesses and industries, moved to different parts of the country, had been married or not married, and had different life experiences. But the students who started off with a clear idea of what they wanted were earning *ten times* as much as those students who started off with just a vague idea of what they wanted to accomplish in life.

Turning Points

Each person has turning points in life, after which she is never the same again. Sometimes these turning points are clear and distinctive. Sometimes they are so subtle that the person does not realize that a major change has taken place in her life until much later.

Brian's first turning point in life was when he discovered that he was *responsible* for his life and for everything that happened to him from that point onward. He learned that this life is not a rehearsal for something else. This is the real thing.

In almost every study of successful, happy people, the acceptance of personal responsibility seems to be the starting point of personal success. Before people accept responsibility, they drift with the tide. Very little happens to them or for them. But after they accept complete responsibility, with no excuses, their whole life begins to change.

When we were children, our parents or legal guardians were largely responsible for taking care of us. They made the decisions that affected our lives. But when we became adults, we were then expected to take care of ourselves. We make our own decisions. We choose our own direction.

The acceptance of complete personal responsibility for your life, and everything that happens to you, can be a scary decision, like parachuting out of an airplane for the first time. But when you accept responsibility, you become an adult for the first time. You become empowered. You feel a tremendous sense of control. Your self-esteem and self-respect soar.

The Biggest Turning Point

The second turning point for Brian, which came when he was twenty-four years old, was his discovery of *goals*. Aside from in sports, he had no idea that goals existed or how to set them. But then he read an article that said, "If you want to be successful, you must have written goals."

His life was going nowhere at that time. He had nothing to lose. So he took out a piece of paper and wrote down ten goals that he wanted to accomplish sometime in the future. He promptly lost the list, but thirty days later, his whole life had changed. Almost every goal on his list had been achieved or partially achieved. It was like a miracle!

Nothing Can Hold You Back

The third turning point in his life came when he discovered that his lack of education or skill did not have to hold him back. He found that he could learn *anything* he needed to learn to accomplish any goal he could set for himself. All business skills, sales skills, and moneymaking skills, even relationship and parenting skills, are *learnable*.

Everyone who is good in any area today was at one time poor in that area. The top people in every field were at one time not even in that field, and didn't even know that field existed. And what hundreds of thousands and millions of other people have done, he could do as well—as can you.

The Goal-Setting Process

Begin by deciding *exactly* what you want in each key area of your life. Idealize, as we have talked about before. Imagine that you have no limitations on what you can be, have, or do. Imagine that you have all the time and money, all the friends and contacts, all the education and experience that you need to accomplish any goals you can set for yourself.

Imagine again that you could wave a magic wand and make your life perfect in each of the four areas of life that we discussed earlier. If your life were perfect in each area, what would it look like, and how would it be different from the way it is today?

1. *Career and profession.* What would be your ideal job, and whom would be your customers? What kind of product or service would you like to offer?

2. *Family.* What kind of lifestyle do you want to create for yourself and your family? What kind of family do you want to have?

3. *Health.* How would your health be different if it were perfect in every way? How would your body feel? What physical activities would you engage in?

4. *Net worth and income.* How much do you want to earn? How much do you want to save and accumulate over the course of your working lifetime?

Just imagine that whatever your answers to these questions, they are possible for you. But your answers must be clear, and they must be in writing.

The Quick List Method

Here is an exercise for you. In less than thirty seconds, write down your three most important goals in life right now. Write quickly.

1. _____

2. _____

3. _____

This is called the Quick List Method of setting goals. When you only have thirty seconds to write down your three most important goals, your answers will be as accurate as if you had thirty minutes or three hours. And whatever you wrote down is probably an accurate description of what you really want in life and what is possible for you.

Describe Your Goals

Your goals must be in writing. They must be clear, specific, detailed, and measurable. You must write out each goal as if you were placing an order for your goal to be manufactured in a factory at a great distance and then sent to you in the mail. Make your description clear and detailed in every sense.

Set Clear Deadlines

Set deadlines for the accomplishment of your goals. Your subconscious mind uses deadlines as "forcing systems" to drive you, to motivate you consciously and unconsciously toward achieving your goals on schedule.

If a goal is big enough, set subdeadlines. If you want to achieve financial independence, for example, you may set a ten- or twenty-year goal and then break it down year by year so that you know how much you have to save and invest each year.

If for some reason you don't achieve your goal by your deadline, simply set a new deadline. There are no unreasonable goals, only unreasonable deadlines.

Identify the Obstacles

Identify the obstacles that you will have to overcome to achieve each goal. It is helpful for you to ask, "Why aren't I already at my goal?"

For example, if your goal is to double your income over the next two or three years, why aren't you *already* earning twice as much? When you ask yourself this question, answers will jump into your mind, some of them accurate and some of them inaccurate. Some of them may just be excuses.

The Theory of Constraints

The theory of constraints says that one limiting factor or constraint sets the *speed* at which you achieve a goal. One choke point or bottleneck is holding you back more than anything else. What is it for you?

The 80/20 Rule applies to constraints. Fully 80 percent of the reasons that are holding you back from achieving your goal are *inside yourself*. They may include the lack of a personal skill, an essential quality, or a body of knowledge. Only 20 percent of the reasons that you are not achieving your goal are on the *outside*. To identify what is holding you back, you should always start with yourself.

The Lure of the Comfort Zone

One major limiting factor is the lure of the comfort zone. Whenever you choose to do something new and different, you are forcing yourself to step outside of your comfort zone, that area of your life and work that is known and familiar. Your comfort zone can be the biggest enemy of your success and achievement.

Sometimes, your comfort zone serves a purpose. When you find yourself struggling to move forward, to set and achieve a new goal, ask yourself, "What purpose does staying in my comfort zone serve?" You may have a fear of failure or rejection. You may feel insecure about your knowledge or ability. Identifying what is keeping you from making a total commitment to something new and different can enable you to get out of your comfort zone and start moving forward.

The comfort zone is also an enemy of balance. Its lure is powerful. It sucks you in and holds you back. You need strength, courage, and determination to counter its pull and move toward what you want. Breaking free usually requires great commitment and personal strength. This is where personal responsibility kicks in. Only you are responsible for starting the momentum and taking the actions necessary to achieve your goals and create balance in your life.

Identify the Knowledge and Skills You Will Need

Identify the knowledge, information, and skills you will need to achieve your goal. Especially, identify the skills that you will have to develop to achieve success.

The truth is that for you to achieve a goal that you have never achieved before, you must develop a skill that you've never had before. You must become a person who you have never been before. You must develop personal characteristics and qualities that you've never had before. You cannot achieve big goals by remaining on the same level that you are on today.

Keep this in mind: your weakest key skill sets the height of your income and your success. You can make more progress by going to work on the one skill that is holding you back than you can by working on any other skill.

Here is the key question: *What one skill, if you developed and did it in an excellent fashion, would have the greatest positive impact on your life?* For example, if your goal is to double your income in the foreseeable future, ask yourself, "What one skill, if I was absolutely excellent at it, would help me the most to double my income?"

Whatever your answer to that question, write it down, make a plan, and work on developing that skill every single day. Remember, all skills are learnable.

Identify the People Whose Help You Will Need

Identify the people whose help and cooperation you will require to achieve your goal. Make a list of every person in your life whom you will have to work with or work around to achieve your most important goals.

Start with the members of your family, whose cooperation and support you will require. List your boss, coworkers, and subordinates. Especially, identify the customers whose support you will need to sell enough of your product or service to make the kind of money that you desire.

Once you have identified the key people whose help you will require, ask yourself this question: "What's in it for them to help me?" Then resolve to be a "go-giver," rather than a go-getter.

To achieve big goals, you will have to have the help and support of lots of people. One key person at a certain time and place in your life can make all the difference.

The most successful people in every society are those who build and maintain the largest networks of other people they can help and who can help them in return.

Your success in life will be based not only on the people you know but on the people who know you in a positive way.

Make a List of Every Step

Make a list of everything that you will have to do to achieve your goal. Combine the obstacles that you will have to overcome, the knowledge and skills that you will have to acquire, and the people whose cooperation you will need. List every step that you can think of that you will have to follow to ultimately achieve your goal.

As you think of new items, add them to your list until your list is complete.

When you make up a list of all the steps that you will need to take to achieve your goal, you will begin to see that this goal is far more attainable than you thought. As Henry

Ford wrote, "Nothing is particularly hard if you divide it into small parts."

Make a Plan of Action

Organize your list into a plan. You can do this by arranging the steps that you have identified by sequence and priority:

1. *Sequence.* What do you have to do *before* you do something else? Put all the steps in order. Create a checklist of steps for the attainment of any goal that is important to you. It is astonishing how much more you will accomplish, and how much faster you will achieve it, when you have a list of activities properly organized from the first activity through to the last.

2. *Priority.* What is more important and what is less important on your list? Remember, 20 percent of the items on your action list will account for 80 percent of the progress that you make toward the attainment of your goal. Resist the temptation to procrastinate on taking care of the big things, and instead, get started on them immediately.

    To set priorities on your list, select your number one most important task for each day. Look at your list and ask yourself this question: "If I could do only *one* thing on this list before I was called out of town for a month, which *one* activity would I want to get done?"

    Whatever your answer, write "#1" next to that task. This becomes the most important thing you could do that day.

    Then ask yourself, "If I could do only one more thing on this list before I was called out of town for a month, which would be the *second* most important task?" Then write "#2" next to that task.

Keep asking this question: "What is the most valuable use of my time on this list?" Do this repeatedly until you have your seven top tasks, organized by sequence and priority.

The 80/20 Rule says that the first 20 percent of the time that you spend planning your goal and organizing your activities will be worth 80 percent of the time and effort required to achieve the goal. Planning is very important.

Plan each day, week, and month in advance:

- Plan each day the evening before.

- Plan each week the weekend before.

- Plan each month at the beginning of the month.

The more complete and detailed you are when you plan your activities, the more you will accomplish in less time. The rule is that each minute spent in planning saves *ten minutes* in execution. This means that you get a 1,000 percent return on your investment of time in planning your days, weeks, and months in advance.

Earn a 10:1 Payoff
For example, it may require only about ten to twelve minutes for you to plan your entire day by making a list and organizing it by priority. But in so doing, you will save yourself at least two hours of wasted time in accomplishing your objectives and achieving your goals.

Goal-Setting Exercise

Take out a clean sheet of paper and write the word "Goals" at the top of the page along with today's date. Discipline yourself to write out at least *ten goals* that you would like to accomplish in the next year or in the foreseeable future.

Begin each goal with the word "I." Only you can use the word "I" with reference to yourself. Follow the word "I" with an *action verb* that acts as a command from your conscious mind to your subconscious mind. This is how you activate all your mental powers.

Describe your goals in the *present* tense, as though they had already been achieved. For example, if your goal is to earn a certain amount of money in a certain time period, you would say, "I earn this amount of money by this date."

State your goal as though it were already a fact and you are reporting on this fact in retrospect. For example, if your goal is to get a new car, you would say, "I drive such and such a new car by such and such a date."

Finally, when you write down your goals, always write them in the *positive* tense. Instead of writing something like, "I will quit smoking," you would simply say, "I am a nonsmoker."

Always state your goals as though they were *already* a reality, as though you had already accomplished them. This command activates your subconscious and superconscious minds to change your external reality so that it is consistent with your inner commands.

Your Major Definite Purpose

Once you have written out a list of ten goals, ask yourself this question: "If I could wave a magic wand and achieve any goal on this list within twenty-four hours, which one goal would have the *greatest positive impact* on my life?"

Whatever your answer to that question, put a circle around that goal. Then, transfer this goal to the top of a clean sheet of paper.

1. Write out your goal clearly and in detail.

2. Set a deadline on this goal and set subdeadlines if necessary.

3. Identify the obstacles that you will have to overcome to achieve this goal, and identify the most important one, internal or external.

4. Identify the knowledge and skills you will need to achieve your goal and the most important skill that you will have to become excellent at to be successful.

5. Identify the people whose help and cooperation you will require, and think about what you can do to deserve their help.

6. Make a list of everything you will have to do to achieve your goal. Add items to this list as you think of new things to do.

7. Organize your list by sequence and priority, by what you have to do first and by what is most important.

8. Make a plan by organizing your list into steps from the first to the last, and then resolve to take action on your plan every single day.

Once you have reached this stage in goal setting and planning, it is absolutely essential that you take the first step. And you can always see the first step.

Do Just One Thing?

Here is another question you can ask yourself: "If I could do only one thing, all day long, which one activity would contribute the most value to my work and to my goals?"

Once you are clear about your goals and their order of importance, and you are clear about your activities and what you should be doing first, you can then practice focus and concentration.

Focus and Concentration

Focus and concentration are the keys to success. Focus means that you know exactly what you want to accomplish, and concentration requires that you dedicate yourself to doing only those activities that will move you toward your goal.

If you desire to achieve greater balance between your personal and professional lives, as many people do, you will actually have more time for your personal life by focusing single-mindedly on your work during the day. If your goal is to achieve great success in your career, your ability to focus on your most important tasks will result in your producing far more, and earning far more, than other people in your field who waste too much of their time.

When you are clear about your goals and you are taking actions every day to achieve those things that mean the most to you, you will feel powerful and productive most of the time. When you are working toward goals that are important to you, you will be aligned with your values and will feel clear, focused, and in balance.

1. Make out a list of ten goals that you would like to accomplish over the next twelve months. Then, select one goal by asking yourself, "If I could achieve only one goal on this list, which one goal would have the greatest positive impact on my life?"

2. Make a list of everything you could do to achieve your most important goal, and then select the one task or activity that could move you toward that goal faster than anything else you could do. Start on that one task immediately.

CHAPTER SIX

Set Your Priorities and Simplify Your Life

You now know who you are and what you really want in life. It is time for you to organize your life so that you are able to maintain your balance point and enjoy the maximum happiness, joy, and personal satisfaction.

Your life is precious. You want to enjoy every moment of it at the highest level possible. You want to achieve the highest return on the expenditure of your mental, emotional, and physical energies.

Life Management

In this sense, time management is really life management, the management of yourself. The quality of your time management largely determines the quality of your life. What you choose to do, and in what order, and what you choose not to do determine your levels of happiness and satisfaction more than anything else. You will always feel more balanced when your time is spent on achieving goals that matter to you.

The good news is that time management is a skill, like riding a bicycle, that can be learned. No matter what you have done or not done in the past, you can learn to become an excellent time manager and to get the very most out of yourself and life every single day.

As we said at the beginning of this book, everyone today has too much to do and too little time. Like everyone else, you often feel overwhelmed with your duties, tasks, and responsibilities. The challenge for you is to simplify your life in such a way that you spend more time doing the things that are most important to you and less time doing those activities that are not important at all.

To simplify your life and to get more done, you should set *peace of mind* as your highest goal and then organize your life around it. Whatever gives you peace, satisfaction, joy, and the feeling of value and importance is right for you.

Whatever causes you stress, dissatisfaction, unhappiness, or irritation is wrong for you.

You must have the courage to organize your life so that you are doing more and more of the things that give you the greatest joy and satisfaction and less and less of those activities that take away from your joy and satisfaction.

Double Your Productivity

Highly productive and successful people practice a series of rituals every day. Before they go to bed at night and when they get up in the morning, they do certain things in a certain way, very much like preparing a dish with a tested and proven recipe. You must do the same.

One of the rituals of high-performing men and women is planning every day in advance. The starting point of setting priorities and achieving high productivity is to "think on paper"! The saying "When you think it, ink it!" applies here.

Make a List

Make a list of everything that you have to do each day, before you begin your day. Generally, the best time to make out your list is the evening before. This allows your subconscious mind to work on the tasks on your list while you sleep. Very often, you will wake up in the morning with ideas and insights about tasks that you can do more effectively.

However, if you are the kind of person who would sit up at night thinking about your list and the things you need to do, then do not write your list the night before. Instead, write out your list the very first thing in the morning, before you begin work of any kind. Make your list before you check your e-mail or look at your social media. Discipline yourself to do nothing before you have written down what you have to do that day. This is an excellent ritual for you to develop that will virtually assure a more productive day. You can write your list while having your morning coffee or tea. With repetition, it will soon become a new habit.

When new activities come up during the day, before you allow yourself to act impulsively, or become distracted, write them down on your list. When you write them down next to the other things you have to do, they take on a different perspective and often do not seem as important as they did when they first came up.

Increase Your Productivity 25 Percent

Working from a list will increase your productivity by 25 percent or more from the first day that you begin doing it. Over time, by working with a list and with a checklist for each of your projects, you will increase your productivity, performance, and output by 50 to 100 percent.

The most immediate benefit from using a list is that it will give you a tremendous sense of control over your life. By working from a list, you will reduce stress and increase your feelings of personal empowerment.

Set Your Priorities

Once you have made a list of everything that you have to do in the coming day, the next step is for you to set priorities on your list. In more than thirty years of research, writing, and teaching on the subject of time management, Brian has concluded that the setting of priorities lies at the heart of all the books and articles ever written on personal productivity.

Perhaps the best definition of time management is this: "Time management enables you to control the sequence of events." By managing your time and setting priorities, you determine in advance what you will do first, what you will do second, and what you won't do at all. In choosing the sequence of the events in your life, you actually choose everything that happens to you.

And you are always *free to choose*. You are always free to select what you are going to do next and what you are not going to do. In your use of this freedom, you determine the quality of your life today and your future life tomorrow. You determine the actions you will take that are reflective of your values and what matters to you.

Make a Date

One of the things that is really important to Christina is having quality one-on-one time with each member of her family. She makes it a priority to have "dates" with each of her three children and her husband at least once a week. What she has discovered, and this is true for many people, is that by having quality time with her family members, she feels more connected to them, which enables her to be more focused and effective when she is working on her professional goals.

Having a date with each family member is at the top of her list. She knows that when she does not create quality one-on-one time with her family members, she has a hard time balancing her desires to be a good wife and mother and to pursue her professional ambitions without feeling guilty. She also notices that her children and husband are less tolerant of her absence when she spends time on work-related tasks, and that makes her feel distracted. To be the most effective and operate from her balance point Christina needs to invest time and energy with her family before she can invest time and energy on her professional ambitions.

Use the 80/20 Rule

Apply the 80/20 Rule to your list. Remember that 20 percent of your activities will account for 80 percent or more of the results that you achieve. In fact, sometimes the 90/10 Rule applies: if you have a list of ten things that you have to do in a day, one of those items will be more important than the other nine tasks put together.

You are a "choosing organism." You are always making choices based on what is more important to you and what is less important. You will be happy only when your choices and your activities are in harmony with your values and beliefs and with what is really important to you.

Consider the Consequences

Perhaps the most important word in time management is "consequences." Something that is important has serious potential consequences. Something that is unimportant is something that has mild consequences or no consequences at all.

Successful, happy people work on those activities that have the greatest potential consequences for their lives, their work, and their families. Unsuccessful people become preoccupied with activities that have low or no consequences, such as watching television or immersing themselves in social media throughout the day.

The ABCDE Method

Once you have made a list of everything that you have to do in the coming day, use the ABCDE Method to set priorities for the tasks on your list.

Must-Do Tasks

An A task is something that you absolutely must do. Completion or noncompletion of the task has serious consequences. If you don't do this task, and do it on time, your failure to complete it will cause problems and unhappiness in your work and personal life.

What are those items on your list that you absolutely, positively must do to fulfill your responsibilities and to be successful?

Should-Do Tasks

B tasks are those that you should do. These are tasks and activities that you need to get done throughout the day, but there are only mild consequences for completion or non-completion. Most of these tasks can be put off until later, and even until tomorrow.

The rule is that you should never do a B task when you have an A task left undone. What are your B tasks?

Goethe said, "Things that matter most must never be at the mercy of those things that matter least."

Nice-to-Do Tasks

C tasks are those that are nice to do but have no consequences at all. Checking your e-mail, reading the newspaper, chatting with a coworker, or getting a cup of coffee are all nice things to do, but they have no consequences in your life and work. If you did not do them at all, it would make no difference.

Successful, happy, productive people focus on their A tasks almost exclusively throughout the day.

Unsuccessful, unhappy, unproductive, and lower-paid people are continually distracted by "shiny objects," by things that are nice to do or fun to do but have no consequences at all for their career or for their futures.

Tasks That Can Be Delegated

D tasks are those that you delegate. The rule is that you should delegate everything that anyone else can do to free up more time for yourself to work on those tasks that only you can do. This requires people who like to be in control to let go of a little control and trust the task to someone else.

Practice the 70 Percent Rule. If somebody else can do a task 70 percent as well as you, it is a task that should be delegated. Many people become successful because they master certain tasks on the way up. They then make the mistake of falling back into doing the tasks that they mastered that got them promoted in the first place. Don't let this happen to you.

The very best managers and executives and the most productive people are those who are continually thinking, "Who else can I get to do this rather than me?"

Tasks That Can Be Eliminated

An E task is something that you should eliminate altogether. This is a low-value or no-value task or activity that contributes nothing to your life or work. It may be fun and enjoyable to do, and it may be something that you became accustomed to doing in the past, but today it has no value at all.

Here is one of the great rules for success: you can get your life in balance and under control only to the degree to which you *stop* doing things of low value. You cannot get your life in balance by doing more things, by becoming more efficient and productive, and by working longer hours. You can get your life under control only when you say no and stop doing those things of low or no value.

The Most Valuable Use of Your Time

The key question in time management is, What is the most valuable use of your time right now? All the books, articles, courses, and workshops come down to helping you determine the answer to this question.

Whatever your answer, this is what you should be working on at the moment. Completing this task is where you can make the greatest contribution to your organization, to your family, and to yourself. What is your answer?

Zero-Based Thinking

Practice zero-based thinking in every part of your life. This technique comes from zero-based budgeting, in which you analyze your expenditures on a quarterly or annual basis. You then ask not whether you should increase or decrease a particular expenditure but whether you should be spending money in that area at all.

Use the same principle in your personal life and business life. Analyze and evaluate every activity in your life, as well as every past decision, and ask yourself, "Knowing what I now know, is there anything I am doing today that I would not start up again today if I had to do it over?"

Conduct a KWINK Analysis

We call this a KWINK analysis. Keep asking yourself, "Knowing what I now know, is there anything that I would not start doing again if I had the opportunity to start again today?"

This is an extremely liberating question. According to research, fully 70 percent of the choices or decisions you make will turn out to be *wrong* in the fullness of time. The people, situations, and conditions involved will change. What seemed like a good idea at the time you made the decision will turn out to be a not particularly good idea at the present. Refuse to become trapped by your decisions from the past.

Courage Is Essential

It takes tremendous courage for you to admit, on a go-forward basis, that you are not *perfect*. It takes tremendous courage for you to admit, knowing what you now know, that there are things in your life that you would not get into again today if you had it to do over.

Three Important Statements

You can use three statements, in conjunction with zero-based thinking, to remain flexible and effective in every area.

1. *Be prepared to say, "I was wrong!"* It is amazing how many people make a mistake and do or say something that they know to be wrong, but because of their *egos*, they cannot admit it. Since you are going to be wrong 70 percent of the time, the sooner you admit it, the sooner you can correct the situation and get on with the rest of your life.

2. *Be willing to say, "I made a mistake."* Many of the things that you do, especially in business and in your career, will turn out to be mistakes in the fullness of time. There is nothing wrong with this. This is how everyone learns and grows. What is wrong is to refuse to correct a mistake because your ego is so invested in being "right."

    The psychologist Gerald Jampolsky once asked, "Do you want to be right or do you want to be happy?" You have to make this decision for yourself.

3. *Learn to say on a regular basis, "I changed my mind."* It is amazing how many people dig themselves into a hole

of stress, anger, frustration, and dissatisfaction because they are not willing to admit that they have changed their minds.

This is not for you. You must stand back and look at your entire life. Is there anything in your life that you would not get into again today if you had to do it over? If there is, have the courage to admit that you have made a mistake (which all people have done) and then take the necessary steps to change.

Task Completion

Once you have written down everything that you have to do, set priorities on your list, and selected the most important thing that you could do right now, the next step in simplification and time management is for you to begin immediately to work on your most important task. Practice single-minded concentration on one thing—the most important thing—and stay at it until it is 100 percent complete.

All success in life comes from task completion. Only when you start and complete important tasks do you get results, and results are everything.

When you repeatedly switch from working on one task to working on another task, commonly referred to as "multi-tasking," you have to invest a certain amount of time to remember exactly where you were when you last stopped working on that other task. When you switch back, you have to spend a certain amount of time getting organized and prepared to restart the old task.

This switching back and forth can increase the amount of time it takes to do a task by five times, far more than if you disciplined yourself to start on the task and work on it until it is 100 percent complete.

The Power of Concentration

Here's some more good news: Concentrated, focused work on a single task is a major source of energy, enthusiasm, and self-esteem. Closure and completion of a major task increases your personal pride and self-respect and motivates you to do even more high-value work.

Everyone wants to feel like a winner. Everyone wants to enjoy the winning feeling throughout the day. How do you experience the feeling of winning? Simple. *You win!*

The way you generate the winning feeling in yourself is by starting and completing important tasks throughout your day. Each time you complete a task, your brain releases endorphins, which are called nature's "happy drugs." Each time you complete a task, you feel happier. You have more energy. You become more creative. Task completion even affects your personality and makes you more genial and personable. You get all these psychic rewards simply by starting and completing important tasks.

Overcoming Procrastination

Perhaps the greatest obstacle to excellent time management is *procrastination*. It is not that people do not know what to do; it is simply that they have a natural tendency to procrastinate, especially on their most important tasks—those tasks that are important but not urgent.

Here are several simple techniques that you can use to overcome procrastination and develop the habit of getting the job done quickly:

1. *Prepare for your task.* One of the techniques that has been helpful in getting organized to work on a project

is gathering everything together so that it is all in front of you and ready to go. This is the first step. After that, it is easier to take the next step and the next and the step after that.

2. *Set a time limit.* Resolve to work on a major task for fifteen minutes and then quit. By setting a time limit and getting started, you begin to develop forward momentum, and you will often find yourself working longer and longer to get the job done.

3. *Set up a reward structure.* Give yourself a reward for completing part of a job. The psychological impact of this strategy is powerful. You actually shift your attention away from the work, which is causing you to procrastinate, and start to focus on the reward, which motivates you to get started.

4. *Promise others.* Tell someone that you will complete a task by a certain time. Once you have told someone else that you will definitely start and complete a task for him, you will find it much easier to motivate yourself to get the job done.

5. *Practice discipline.* Imagine that you are going to be called out of town for a month unexpectedly. Before you go, you must complete one major task. Which major task would it be? Whatever it is, discipline yourself to start and complete that task as fast as you can.

Resolve today to eliminate procrastination. It has been said that "Procrastination is the thief of time." It is even more accurate to say that "Procrastination is the thief of life."

Fortunately, whatever you do repeatedly soon becomes a new *habit*. When you organize your work and select the most important task that you could do and then start on that task immediately each day, you will soon develop the habit of starting and completing important tasks. Your productivity, performance, and output will all go up. Your self-esteem and self-satisfaction will both increase. When you complete a task, you will feel like a winner. You will earn the esteem and respect of all the people around you. You will get paid more and promoted faster. Your whole life will change when you eliminate the habit of procrastination from your life.

All Skills Are Learnable

Remember, all skills are learnable. You can learn any skill you need to learn to achieve any goal that you set for yourself.

Time management is a skill set that can be learned and that must be learned. You can become a superb time manager by practicing the techniques taught in this chapter and by continually educating yourself on how to be more productive in your work.

The best news is that you could be only one time management skill away from doubling your productivity, performance, and eventually your income. You could be one time management skill away from spending more quality time with family and friends, staying present when it matters, and being engaged in meaningful activities. And as a result of what you have learned in this chapter, you probably know exactly which time management skill can help you the most to make a greater contribution, achieve more success, and experience more balance between your career and your personal life.

You have the ability right now to organize your life around your values, to put your time and energy into those activities that have the most meaning for you and that allow you to achieve all of your personal and professional goals.

~~~~~~~~~~~**ACTION EXERCISES**~~~~~~~~~~~

1. From this day forward, make it a habit—a daily ritual—to plan every day in advance, and always work from your plan.

2. Select your most important task each day, start on that task immediately, and discipline yourself to focus on that one task until it is complete.

CONCLUSION

Four Ways to Energize Your Life

There are only four ways that you can change your life or your work to enable you to stay on track and align with your balance point. They are simple and powerful.

1. *You can do more of some things.* What should you be doing more of if you want to be happier and more effective? The answer is usually that you should be doing more of those things from which you are getting the best results, those things that make you the happiest and that give you the greatest feeling of well-being in your life and work.

2. *You can do less of other things.* What should you be doing less of? Obviously, you should be doing less of the things that are not working for you—that are not giving you good results and are causing you unhappiness and frustration.

3. *You can start doing something that you are not doing today.* This is usually the hardest change to make. For you to start doing something completely new and different requires tremendous discipline and willpower. Everyone slips into a comfort zone, and becomes accustomed to doing certain activities, even if they are no longer working for the person.

What do you need to start doing today to create a wonderful life for yourself at some time in the future? What new activities do you need to engage in? What new subjects do you need to learn? What new goals do you need to set for yourself and work on every day?

4. *You can stop doing certain things altogether.* This brings us back to zero-based thinking. What are those things in your life that you should discontinue altogether so that you have more time to do the activities that are really important to you?

In time management and personal management, and whenever you feel frustrated or unhappy for any reason, ask yourself this great question: *"What should I do more of, do less of, start, or stop?"* You will always find the answers somewhere within yourself.

When you begin to follow these ideas each day, you will find your balance point, your center, and begin to achieve all the wonderful things that are possible you.

Good luck!

ACKNOWLEDGMENTS

Both Brian and I would like to acknowledge and thank the wonderful team at Berrett-Koehler, especially our wonderful publisher, Steve Piersanti; our editor, Jeevan Sivasubramaniam, and BK's vice president of sales and marketing, Kristen Frantz.

I would like to thank my husband, Damon, for his love and support while I was writing this book. He has been an incredible unofficial editor and supporter of this process. I would also like to thank my dad and coauthor of this book. Dad, I really appreciate your teaching me to fish and then trusting me to do the fishing. It's been a real joy working with you and learning from you. You have always supported and believed in me, and that has had such an impact on my ability to visualize a life with boundless possibility. I would also like to thank my kids, Julia, Will, and Scarlett, for being patient with me when I had to go to work and finish all my "homework."

I couldn't have written this book if I didn't have the support of other women to care for my kids when I was focusing on my professional ambitions, and so I'd also like to thank Jai Lust, Angelica Donis, Maria Contreras, and all my

Acknowledgments

"mommy" friends who stepped in when I needed help. I hope that more and more women will support each other to fulfill their potential and achieve balance in their lives.

CHRISTINA STEIN

INDEX

identity, professional, 39–40
identity values, 20–22
"I'll try" versus "I will," 45
imagining your future, 30
    clarity for achieving, 37
    first step to, 44
    leadership of your life for,
        38–48
    magic question for, 38
    no limitations for, 36
    perfect job, 53–57
    See also career visioning;
    vision creation/visualization
inner experience, 3
interpretation of experiences,
    46–47
investments, financial, 42–43

J
jobs, 39–40, 53–57, 64
"just one thing" question,
    74

K
knowledge, identifying
    needed, 68
KWINK analysis, 85

L
Law of Attraction, 49
Law of Correspondence, 36, 49
lawyer/salesman examples,
    23–24
leadership of your life,
    38
learning experiences, 47

life
    deserving your, 52–53
    energizing your, 93–94
    finding your purpose in,
        51–52
    ideal (*see* imagining your
        future)
    living by accident or design,
        43
    living to work, 55
    managing your, 77–78
    meaning of (*see* meaning of/
        in life)
life values, 19–20
limitations/limiting beliefs,
    33, 36
list-making, 40, 65, 68–70,
    79–80

M
magic question for vision
    creation, 38
making lists, 40, 65, 68–70,
    79–80
meaning of/in life
    accepting responsibility for
        your life, 63
    deserving your life, 52–53
    exercises for finding, 59
    family/friends/community,
        57–59
    finding your perfect job,
        53–57
    looking into yourself, 58–59
    reason for existence, 51–52
mistakes, 86

SERVICES OFFERED

Brian Tracy
Speaker, Consultant, Executive Coach

Brian Tracy is one of the top professional speakers in the world, addressing more than 250,000 people each year throughout the United States, Europe, Asia, and Australia. His keynote speeches, talks, and seminars are described as "inspiring, entertaining, informative, and motivational." His audiences include businesses and associations of every size and type, including many Fortune 500 companies. Since he began speaking professionally, Brian has shared his ideas with more than five million people in seventy countries and has served as a consultant and trainer for more than one thousand corporations. Some of his topics include the following:

21st Century Thinking
How to outthink, outperform, outsell, and outstrategize your competition to get superior results in a turbulent, fast-changing business environment.

Leadership in the New Millennium
How to apply the most powerful leadership principles ever discovered to manage, motivate, and get better results, faster than ever before.

Advanced Selling Strategies
How to outthink, outperform, and outsell your competition using the most advanced strategies and tactics known to modern selling.

The Power of Personal Productivity
How to get organized, set clear priorities, focus on key tasks, overcome procrastination, concentrate single-mindedly on your most important tasks, and get more done in a day than many people get done in a week. You learn the strategies and techniques of the most productive people in every field.

For full information on booking Brian to speak at your next meeting or conference, visit Brian Tracy International at www.briantracy.com, or call (858) 436-7300 for a free promotional package. Brian will carefully customize his talk for you and for your needs.

The Two-Day MBA
Brian Tracy's Total Business Mastery Seminar
(Two-Day Live Seminar/Workshop)
In this two-day Total Business Mastery Seminar, Brian Tracy will give you a practical and immediately actionable, street-smart MBA. You will learn the ten most powerful and important principles for business success, which you can put to work the next day.

Throughout this two-day program, you will work through an action guide and eye-opening exercises that will enable you to apply every idea to your own business, sometimes before the seminar is over. You'll work on your business and mastermind with your peers about your strengths, weaknesses, challenges, and greatest opportunities. You'll leave this seminar with a written plan to increase your sales, reduce your costs, and boost your profits.

You learn how to become a more effective executive and generate the critical numbers essential for business success.

You learn and internalize the ten great areas of business success, becoming one of the best businesspeople in your industry.

This entire program can be presented, with all materials, to individuals, corporations, and organizations of almost any size.

For more information
go to www.briantracy.com/tbm
or call (858) 436-7300

Learn the practical, proven skills and techniques that you need to survive, thrive, and grow in any business and in any market.

Christina Stein, MA, MFT
Speaker, Author, Therapist

Christina Stein is a speaker, author, and psychotherapist who focuses on work-life balance and female empowerment. She spends her time advising individuals and couples as well as conducting workshops to help attendees align their priorities and goals with their skills and passions. Christina is based in Los Angeles and works internationally. She combines her training as a marriage and family therapist with her experience as a life coach to work empathically and dynamically with her clients, facilitating rapid growth and transformation.

Christina offers two exciting workshops:

Let Out the Lioness—targeted toward women

This workshop is designed for women who are caught in the whirlwind of trying to excel personally and professionally while being present at home with their children and attentive and nurturing toward their partner. With so much focus on maintaining the world around them, women too often lose touch with themselves and forget to nurture their own sexuality.

In this workshop, Christina teaches participants how to awaken their desire, giving them greater self-confidence and empowering them as women. Participants explore ways to create greater intimacy with their partner and to light a spark that will bring back the excitement and anticipation in their relationship.

Find Your Balance Point—targeted toward men and women

People experience true balance when they find and operate from their balance point, which is unique to each individual. It is from this balance point that individuals experience the highest level of clarity, commitment, strength, and confidence to pursue their ambitions, personally and professionally. The key to happiness, fulfillment, and success in any area of life is to start from the right place—one's personal balance point—and to be guided and powered by this clarity and commitment.

This workshop is designed to help participants achieve their version of work-life balance. Christina teaches participants how to create a life plan and operate from a place of balance, strength, and clarity. She guides participants to discover their life's values, vision, and purpose and to set goals that enable each person to reach his or her potential.

**For more information
go to www.christinatracystein.com
or call (310) 749-7622.**

ABOUT THE AUTHORS

 **Brian Tracy** is chairman and CEO of Brian Tracy International, a company specializing in the training and development of individuals and organizations. He is among the top speakers, trainers, and seminar leaders in the world today.

Brian has consulted for more than one thousand large companies and addressed more than five million people in five thousand talks and seminars throughout the United States, Canada, and seventy other countries worldwide. As a keynote speaker and seminar leader, he addresses more than two hundred and fifty thousand people each year.

He has studied, researched, written, and spoken for thirty years in the fields of economics, history, business, philosophy, and psychology. He is the top-selling author of seventy books that have been translated into forty-two languages.

Brian has written and produced more than eight hundred audio and video learning programs, including the worldwide best-selling *Psychology of Achievement*, which has been translated into twenty-eight languages.

He speaks to corporate and public audiences on the subjects of personal and professional development, including the executives and staffs of many of America's largest corporations. His exciting talks and seminars on business success, leadership, strategic selling, self-esteem, goals, strategy, creativity, and success psychology bring about immediate changes and long-term results.

Prior to founding Brian Tracy International, Brian was the chief operating officer of a $265 million development company. He has had successful careers in sales and marketing, investments, real estate development and syndication, importation, distribution, and management consulting. He has conducted high-level consulting assignments with several billion-dollar corporations in strategic planning and organizational development.

He has traveled and worked in more than one hundred countries on six continents and speaks four languages. Brian is happily married with four children. He is active in community and national affairs and is the president of three companies headquartered in Solana Beach, California.

Brian is the president of Business Growth Strategies, an Internet-based company that helps businesses of all sizes increase their sales and profitability by implementing the best practices of top businesses worldwide.

To learn more about Brian Tracy, please visit his website at www.briantracy.com.

Christina Stein has spent her whole life being driven by the desire to help others experience authenticity, connection, and personal and professional empowerment. She began to pursue this quest by earning her master's degree in clinical psychology from Antioch University and then becoming licensed as a marriage and family therapist. She has been in private practice since 2005 and has an office in Santa Monica, California. She believes that when people are helped to understand and appreciate their feelings, they can learn to live authentic lives, develop stronger boundaries, and feel more confident to pursue their goals and ambitions.

Christina is passionate about the value of feeling both emotionally and physically connected to our partners and ourselves. She has three young children and has been with her husband for seventeen years. Through her personal experiences and professional endeavors, she has developed great compassion regarding the need for loving, connected relationships. For the last seven years she has been researching, developing, and facilitating her workshop designed to empower individuals in their sexuality, create enthusiasm and intimacy in their relationships, and take the monotony out of monogamy. She also works with individuals and couples as a sex coach and helps them realize and appreciate the potential of their sexuality. She is a sex expert and graduate of Sex Coach U, a sex educator, and a certified clinical sexologist. She is currently pursuing her doctorate in human sexuality from the Institute for Advanced Study of Human Sexuality.

Growing up the daughter of a motivational speaker, Christina was naturally compelled to want to empower others personally and professionally. She has trained extensively with her father, Brian Tracy, and has learned a tremendous amount about personal and professional development. She and Brian coauthored a previous book, which has been published in more than a dozen countries. Christina is also a life coach and works individually with people and speaks to groups on how to discover their values, vision, purpose, and goals. She teaches them essential techniques to manage their time and live a life in balance with meaning and purpose.

To learn more about Christina Stein, please visit her website at www.christinatracystein.com.

Also by Brian Tracy and Christina Stein

Kiss That Frog!

12 Great Ways to Turn Negatives into Positives in Your Life and Work

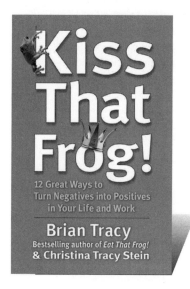

Negative thoughts and emotions are the number-one reason people don't fulfill their potential. The good news is that you have the power to change this. You can "kiss" your negative "frogs" and transform them into positives. The many powerful techniques and exercises in this book will help you change your mindset so that you discover something worthwhile in every person and experience, however difficult and challenging they might seem at first. You'll learn how to turn problems into benefits, develop unshakable self-confidence, become your best self, and begin living an extraordinary life.

Hardcover, 168 pages, ISBN 978-1-60994-280-9
PDF ebook, ISBN 978-1-60994-281-6

Berrett–Koehler Publishers, Inc.
www.bkconnection.com   **800.929.2929**

Also by Brian Tracy

Eat That Frog!
21 Great Ways to Stop Procrastinating and Get More Done in Less Time, Second Edition

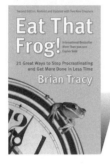

There's an old saying that if the first thing you do each morning is to eat a live frog, you'll have the satisfaction of knowing that you've done the hardest thing you'll do all day. Using this as a metaphor for tackling difficult tasks that you are most likely to put off but that can have the greatest positive impact on your life, Brian Tracy shows you how to not only get more done but get the *right* things done.

Paperback, 144 pages, ISBN 978-1-57675-422-1
PDF ebook, ISBN 978-1-57675-504-4

Goals!
How to Get Everything You Want—Faster Than You Ever Thought Possible, Second Edition

Brian Tracy presents a simple, powerful, and effective system for setting and achieving goals—a method that has been used by more than one million people to achieve extraordinary things. In this revised and expanded second edition, he has added three new chapters addressing areas in which goals can be most rewarding but also the toughest to set and keep: finances, family, and health.

Paperback, 304 pages, ISBN 978-1-60509-411-3
PDF ebook, ISBN 978-1-60509-412-0

BK Berrett–Koehler Publishers, Inc.
www.bkconnection.com   **800.929.2929**

Also by Brian Tracy

Flight Plan
The Real Secret of Success

Life is a journey, and as with any other journey you need clear goals, plans, and schedules to get from where you are now to where you want to be—a flight plan. In this powerful, practical book, Brian Tracy uses the metaphor of an airplane trip to help you chart a course to greater achievement, happiness, and personal fulfillment.

Hardcover, 168 pages, ISBN 978-1-57675-497-9
Paperback, ISBN 978-1-60509-275-1
PDF ebook, ISBN 978-1-57675-556-3

The 100 Absolutely Unbreakable Laws of Business Success

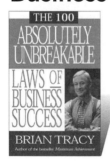

Why are some people more successful in business than others? Why do some businesses flourish where others fail? In this eye-opening practical guide, Brian Tracy presents a set of universal laws that lie behind the success of businesspeople everywhere. He provides numerous real-life examples to illustrate how each law functions and practical guidance and exercises for applying each to your life and work.

Paperback, 336 pages, ISBN 978-1-57675-126-8
PDF ebook, ISBN 978-1-57675-794-9

Berrett–Koehler Publishers, Inc.
www.bkconnection.com

800.929.2929

Also by Brian Tracy

Be a Sales Superstar

21 Great Ways to Sell More, Faster, Easier in Tough Markets

Based on his close work with top salespeople and his keen observation of their methods, as well as his own experiences as a record-breaking salesman, Brian Tracy presents key ideas and techniques that address both the *inner* game of selling (the mental component) and the *outer* game of selling (the methods and techniques of actually making the sale).

Paperback, 168 pages, ISBN 978-1-57675-273-9
PDF ebook, ISBN 978-1-60509-836-4

The 21 Success Secrets of Self-Made Millionaires

How to Achieve Financial Independence Faster and Easier Than You Ever Thought Possible

Brian Tracy shows how anyone, no matter where he or she is in life at this moment, can become a millionaire. The advice in this book is based on Tracy's decades of careful analysis of the habits and practices of hundreds of self-made millionaires, as well as his own rags-to-riches experience. A net worth of $1,000,000? Why not you?

Hardcover, 96 pages, ISBN 978-1-58376-205-9
PDF ebook, ISBN 978-1-57675-918-9

BK® Berrett–Koehler Publishers, Inc.
www.bkconnection.com   **800.929.2929**

Also by Brian Tracy

Get Paid More and Promoted Faster

21 Great Ways to Get Ahead in Your Career

Brian Tracy reveals how you can apply the secrets and strategies used by the highest-paid people in our society to maximize your own strengths, make yourself more valuable, and become virtually indispensable to your company. This book will help you develop the discipline and determination you need to get more done, earn the respect of coworkers and bosses, and move upward to greater and greater levels of success.

Hardcover, 128 pages, ISBN 978-1-58376-207-3
PDF ebook, ISBN 978-1-57675-802-1

Hire and Keep the Best People

21 Practical and Proven Techniques You Can Use Immediately

From corner cubicle to corporate suite, managers today say their biggest concern is the competition for talent, yet most managers have never received any formal training in the process of personnel selection. In a single brief volume, Brian Tracy draws on decades of training managers in the art of employee selection to pinpoint the twenty-one most important, proven principles of employee recruitment and retention.

Hardcover, 144 pages, ISBN 978-1-57675-169-5
PDF ebook, ISBN 978-1-60994-186-4

BK® Berrett–Koehler Publishers, Inc.
www.bkconnection.com   800.929.2929

Berrett–Koehler
Publishers

Berrett-Koehler is an independent publisher dedicated to an ambitious mission: *connecting people and ideas to create a world that works for all*.

We believe that to truly create a better world, action is needed at all levels—individual, organizational, and societal. At the individual level, our publications help people align their lives with their values and with their aspirations for a better world. At the organizational level, our publications promote progressive leadership and management practices, socially responsible approaches to business, and humane and effective organizations. At the societal level, our publications advance social and economic justice, shared prosperity, sustainability, and new solutions to national and global issues.

A major theme of our publications is "Opening Up New Space." Berrett-Koehler titles challenge conventional thinking, introduce new ideas, and foster positive change. Their common quest is changing the underlying beliefs, mindsets, institutions, and structures that keep generating the same cycles of problems, no matter who our leaders are or what improvement programs we adopt.

We strive to practice what we preach—to operate our publishing company in line with the ideas in our books. At the core of our approach is stewardship, which we define as a deep sense of responsibility to administer the company for the benefit of all of our "stakeholder" groups: authors, customers, employees, investors, service providers, and the communities and environment around us.

We are grateful to the thousands of readers, authors, and other friends of the company who consider themselves to be part of the "BK Community." We hope that you, too, will join us in our mission.

A BK Life Book

This book is part of our BK Life series. BK Life books change people's lives. They help individuals improve their lives in ways that are beneficial for the families, organizations, communities, nations, and world in which they live and work. To find out more, visit **www.bk-life.com**.

Berrett–Koehler
Publishers

Connecting people and ideas
to create a world that works for all

Dear Reader,

Thank you for picking up this book and joining our worldwide community of Berrett-Koehler readers. We share ideas that bring positive change into people's lives, organizations, and society.

To welcome you, we'd like to offer you a free e-book. You can pick from among twelve of our bestselling books by entering the promotional code **BKP92E** here: http://www.bkconnection.com/welcome.

When you claim your free e-book, we'll also send you a copy of our e-newsletter, the *BK Communiqué*. Although you're free to unsubscribe, there are many benefits to sticking around. In every issue of our newsletter you'll find

- A free e-book
- Tips from famous authors
- Discounts on spotlight titles
- Hilarious insider publishing news
- A chance to win a prize for answering a riddle

Best of all, our readers tell us, "Your newsletter is the only one I actually read." So claim your gift today, and please stay in touch!

Sincerely,

Charlotte Ashlock
Steward of the BK Website

Questions? Comments? Contact me at bkcommunity@bkpub.com.

Certified

Corporation™
bcorporation.net